KB264951

빛을 따라 걸었더니
아름다운 추억

Walking After the Light
Beautiful Memories

여귀옥 대성그룹 명예회장 회고록
Memoirs of Kwi Ok Yeu
Honorary Chairwoman of the Daesung Group

대성그룹 창립 60주년 기념 출판

여귀옥 대성그룹 명예회장 회고록

빛을 따라 걸었더니

아름다운 추억

JCR

Mother

(May 10, 1985)

Like the blooming bud of a pink rose,
Drizzled with the early morning dew
In a summer garden,

My gracefully beautiful
And noble mother
Overflows with God's sweet scent of blessings.

*(Written for Mother on her birthday
by Younghoon while at Harvard University)*

Proverbs 31 portrays a virtuous woman of noble character. My mother lived a life that was humble and God-fearing, wise and holy, loving and victorious, by the grace of our Lord Jesus Christ, who walked with her all her days.

With the guidance of the Holy Spirit, she developed a fervent passion for evangelism. She spent many days recounting the countless blessings she received from God, and she managed to leave us with the gift of an autobiography titled *Beautiful Memories*. The book was

을 남겨 주셨다. 이 글은 1993년 어머님의 칠순 때 출판
된 후 한국판은 5쇄를 넘기면서, 읽는 사람들마다 성령 충
만한 은혜를 받고 그리스도 앞으로 나오게 했다. 영어로
도 재판이 나와서 영어권의 많은 독자들의 삶에 축복이 되
었고, 특히 35개국 절제회원들이 읽고 많은 은혜를 받고
있다.

어머님 자서전은 꼭 '천로역정' 같이 하나님의 역사를
정리하고 있다. 어머님의 자서전을 요약하여 어머님의 믿
음과 사랑, 그리고 절제의 열매를 풍성히 맺으시며 살아가
신 승리의 삶을 널리 나누려고 한다. 이 회고록을 읽는 모
든 독자들이 예수 그리스도를 믿고 어머님처럼 아브라함
의 복을 받게 되시기를 기도드린다.

2007년 5월 10일 대성그룹 60주년에

둘째 딸 김정주 박사

연세대학교 교수

대성닷컴 사장

first published in 1993, when Mother celebrated her 70th birthday, and it has since reached its fifth printing in Korean and second in English. Many who read Mother's memoirs were filled with the power of the Holy Spirit, and many more have come to believe in Christ. The English translation of *Beautiful Memories* has also blessed the lives of many English-speaking readers, especially World Woman's Christian Temperance Union members throughout its thirty-five affiliated countries.

Like John Bunyan's *Pilgrim's Progress*, my mother's memoirs give a genuine account of God's history. In publishing this condensed version of *Beautiful Memories*, I hope to spread news of the victorious life my mother lived in love and faith, and of the fruit of temperance she bore. I pray that all who read her memoirs may believe in Jesus Christ and receive the blessings of Abraham.

Dr. Jung Joo Kim
Professor, Yonsei University
President, Daesung.com
In celebration of the 60th anniversary of the Daesung Group
May 10, 2007

● 목 차

Foreword

Chapter 1
Love is Patient
사랑은
오래 참고

대성그룹 김수근 창업회장과 여귀옥 명예회장
Founding Chairman of the Daesung Group, Mr. Soo Keun Kim,
and Honorary Chairwoman Mrs. Kwi Ok Yeu (1986)

저자의 어머니 최성연 권사
My mother, Elderwoman
Sung Nyun Choi

여학교 시절의 저자
School years (1937)

신혼 시절
Recently
married (1941)

즐거운 여름 돈암장
With husband in summer at
Don Am Jang (1963)

1. 나의 부모님

나는 1923년 5월 10일, 아버님 여용섭 장립 집사님과 어머님 최성연 권사님의 5남 1녀 중에서 귀염둥이 외동딸로 태어났다. 나의 어머님은 성경 선생님으로서 선교사님들과 늘 동행하였고, 경북 일대에서 성령충만한 집회를 자주 인도하셨다. 선교사님들은 어머님을 '가브리엘'이라고 부르시며, 기쁜 소식을 전하는 사자라고 존경하고 사랑했다. 내가 자라나던 우리 가정에서는 아침 6시가 되면 온 식구가 안방에 모여서 가정예배를 드렸다.

어릴 때 기억으로, 어머님께서 성경책을 들고 설교를 시작하시면 온 청중이 은혜를 받고 청년이나 노년이나 모두 성령의 충만함을 받았다. 어머님은 신구약을 거의 다 외우고 계셔서 누가 질문을 해도 막히는 일이 없으셨다. 지금까지도 교인들은 어머님이 은혜롭게 하나님의 말씀을 가르치시던 모습을 기억한다. 나는 학교에서 수업과 클럽 활동이 늦게 끝나는 날이면 으레 교회에 가서 어머님을 뵙곤 했다. 우리 교회에서는 일 년 열두 달 내내 성경 공부가 계속되고 있었다. 어머님은 중요한 성경 구절, 예를 들어 성경 전체를 요약하는 요한복음 3:16을 늘 외우라고 말씀하셨다.

1. My Parents

I was born in Daegu, Korea, on May 10, 1923, as the dearly beloved only daughter of six children. My father, Yong Sup Yeu, was an esteemed deacon; my mother, Sung Nyun Choi, was an elderwoman. Mother led Bible study groups and gatherings with American Presbyterian Church missionaries. She also led many Holy Spirit–filled meetings in Gyeong-sangbuk-do, which is located in the southeastern part of Korea. The missionaries loved her and respected her as one who always preached the Good News. Gabriel was what they called her. Growing up, our family always gathered at six o'clock every morning to have a family worship service.

All the church members, young and old alike, were abundantly blessed by the Lord through my mother's Bible study groups. Because she studied the Bible so diligently, she knew most Bible verses by heart from the Old and New Testaments and could answer all questions without hesitation. Even to this day, her former students and our church members remember how graceful she was when teaching the Word of God. Whenever I was late leaving school or my after-school lessons, I would go to church to meet up with my mother, who would, as always, be in Bible study class. At our church, Bible study classes ran all throughout the year. Mother urged me to memorize Bible passages, such as John 3:16.

나는 어머님께서 가르쳐 주시는 성경 구절을 모두 순종해서 외웠다. 로마서 8장은 너무 길어서 지금도 다 못 외우는데 어머님은 아침마다 이 장을 외우셨다. 나는 어머님을 사랑했다. 내가 어릴 적부터 나를 안으시고는 성경에 나오는 에스더와 같은 사람이 되라고 말씀하셨다. 어릴 적부터 부모님께 순종하여 배운 하나님의 말씀은 일생 동안 나에게 마음의 등불이 되어, 이 험한 세상을 행복하게 살아갈 수 있도록 했다. 또한 나의 자녀들에게도 항상 어머님의 교육을 본받아 먼저 성경 말씀을 많이 봉독하고 암송하도록 권한다.

어머님은 내가 어렸을 때에 태교에 대해 말씀해 주셨다. 나를 태 중에 가지고 계실 때에 잔칫집에 간 적이 있으셨다. 다들 술을 마시라고 권했다. 어머님은 마시고 싶은 마음이 생리적으로 더했다. 그러나 하나님께 기도를 드렸다. "내가 지금 한 생명을 잉태했는데 만약 술을 마시고 한 생명에게 나쁜 영향을 끼치면 하나님께 얼마나 큰 죄를 범하는 것입니까? 이것을 안 먹고 참을 수 있도록 해 주시옵소서." 하고 말이다. 어머

I memorized all the passages she told me to learn by heart. While I still haven't memorized all of Romans 8, Mother recited this entire chapter every morning. I loved my mother. When I was a child, she often held me in her arms, telling me to become like Esther from the Bible. All the lessons from the Bible that I learned from my parents when I was young have now become a light in my mind and have helped me to lead a blessed and joyous life, even through the rough times. Following my mother's example, I now encourage my children to meditate upon God's Word and to memorize Scripture verses.

My mother told me what great precautions she took during her pregnancies. While pregnant with me, she was invited to a wedding. Everyone tried to talk her into drinking some wine, making it more difficult since she already had a craving for it. In the midst of all this, she prayed to God: "O, Lord! If I drink while pregnant, the baby in my womb will be harmed, and what a great sin that would be! Lord, help me overcome this strong desire." Mother told me, "I resisted my desire to drink the wine, so that I would give birth to a wonderful, healthy child. Please become a great woman like Esther from

님은 "착하고 건강한 아기를 낳기 위해 술을 마시지 않았다. 너는 부디 에스더와 같이 귀한 사람이 되어다오." 하시면서 내게 늘 부탁하셨다.

어머님은 딸 하나를 두시고 내가 어릴 때부터 좋은 배필을 만나게 해 달라고 하나님께 늘 기도드리며 축복하셨다. 이와 같은 어머님의 기도로 나는 일생 고생을 모르고 살고 있다. 나의 어머님은 모든 일을 하나님께 기도드린 다음 시작하셨고, 항상 가난한 자들을 도와 주셨다.

어머님께서는 시골에서 부흥회를 인도하시고 집에 돌아오시면 언제나 우리 6남매를 다 키우시고 결혼시킨 후에 당신은 하나님의 어린 양떼들을 돌보시면서 여생을 보내겠다고 말씀하셨다. 정말 당신이 원하시던 대로 우리들을 다 성혼시킨 후에 농촌의 어린 양떼들을 돌보셨다. 마지막에 경북 의성교회를 섬기다가 넘어지셔서 집으로 모시고 왔는데 그 길로 몇 년 후 세상을 떠나셨다. 병상에 계실 때에도 많은 성도들이 병문안을 오시면 어머님이 어찌나 기쁨으로 충만하셨던지, 어머님을 위로하러 오셨던 분들이 오히려 위로를 받고 은혜를 풍성히 받아 돌아가시곤 했다.

어머님이 세상을 떠나시니 외동딸로서 받은 그 많은 사랑만큼 마음이 슬펐다. 어머님이 소천하신 지 3개월 후, 하루는

the Bible."

Because I was the only daughter, my mother prayed for my future husband ever since I was just a child. Thanks to her prayers, God blessed me with a wonderful husband and family. My mother always prayed to God before she did anything; she always helped the poor and unfortunate.

Whenever Mother returned home from revival meetings in the countryside, she would tell me and my brothers that she would dedicate her life to taking care of God's little lambs that lived in the poverty-stricken countryside when she was done raising us. After all of us children married, she spent the rest of her life ministering to the poor, just as she had wished. While working as an evangelist at Euisung Presbyterian Church, she had a stroke. After six years of being bedridden, she went to be with the Lord. While Mother was ill, many brothers and sisters in Christ came to comfort her. All who came to comfort my mother were, instead, comforted by her, because she was filled with the Holy Spirit.

After Mother passed away, I, being the only daughter, felt great sorrow because I loved her so dearly. One day about three months after my mother's death, I was in a state of semiconsciousness when I saw a vision of my mother rising from her coffin. She was wearing a shining white dress with beautiful embroidery. I asked her, "Mother! How is it possible that you are ascending?" Mother answered, "My

비몽사몽 간에 아름다운 무늬가 수 놓인 흰 옷을 입으신 어머님이 관에서 일어나고 계셨다. 내가 "어머님! 돌아가셨는데 어떻게 일어나십니까?"하고 여쭈었더니, "아가야! 나는 천국에 있다. 기뻐해라." 하시면서 웃으셨다. 그때에 나는 너무도 기뻤다. 그리스도의 부활의 증거를 나는 보았다. 그 후로 나는 더 이상 슬퍼하지 않았다.

어머님

흰 모시 단정하게 입으신 그 모습이
아직도 이 눈에 선명히 떠오른다
저 멀리 가신 어머님 오늘 밤도 그리워

일생을 아름답게 살으신 그 모습이
갈수록 이 마음에 영롱히 비치누나
조용히 미소 지으시던 인자하신 그 얼굴

거룩한 그 발자욱 헛되지 않아
알알이 열매 맺어 주님을 찬양하네
성경을 손에 들고 미개한 우리 농촌
불쌍해 애태우시며 계몽길 다니시던
거룩한 그 발자욱은 헛되지 않았지

child, I have entered into heaven. Rejoice!" as she smiled. I was truly happy; I have not grieved over her death since.

Mother

The image of you wearing a white ramie dress
Still appears vividly before my eyes.
Tonight, as always, I miss you, Mother.

The image of you, who led such a beautiful life,
Shines more gloriously as time passes by.
I miss your radiant face, your quiet smile,
and your steadfast love.

Your holy footsteps were not in vain;
One by one, they each bore fruit and praised the Lord.
You held a Bible in your hand; and full of compassion,
To the dark countryside you went to raise them up.
Your holy footsteps were never in vain.

Mother, you always showed so much compassion
for our nation,
A nation that suffered from physical and
spiritual warfare.

영육간 가난한 채 지내는 내 민족이
언제나 어머님은 불쌍하고 애달파서
우리들 다 키우시고 그들 위해 살리라
수시로 말씀하셨지

숭고한 그 정신은 다음날 열매 맺어
병들어 쓰러지실 때까지 농촌 위해 일하셨네

나의 아버님 여용섭 장립 집사님은 1877년 이 땅에 태어나셨다. 아버님은 사업가이셨는데 선한 마음으로 어머님의 복음 전도 활동을 성심껏 뒷받침해 주셨다. 아버님은 예수님을 믿기 전에는 술도 드신 모양이다. 어머님이 진실하게 믿으시고 한결같이 선한 성품으로 내조하시는 것에 감동을 받아 아버님도 믿으시게 되었다.

그때만 해도 기독교가 들어온 지 몇십 년 못 되어서, 남자들은 거의 다 술을 많이 마셨다. 자녀들의 교육도 돌보지 않고 가산이 탕진 되는 것도 모르고 음주에 빠져 있었다. 그래서 우리는 어릴 때 이런 노래를 부르면서 행진한 기억이 난다.

"아- 마시지 마라, 그 술!
아- 보지도 마라, 그 술!
조선 사회 복 받기는 금주함에 있느니라."

You often said you would live for the poor
After you were done raising us, your children.

Your lofty vision later bore fruit.
You continued to labor for the people in the countryside
Until illness took away your health.

My father, Deacon Yong Sup Yeu, was born in 1877 in Korea. He was a kind businessman who wholeheartedly supported my mother in her ministry to preach the Gospel. Before he accepted Christ into his life, he occasionally drank alcohol. Moved by my mother's sincere faith and goodness in Christ, Father came to believe in Christ.

Since Christianity had been introduced to this nation only a few decades earlier, many men in Korea drank a great deal of alcohol. Many of them ended up neglecting their children's need for education and wasted all their money on alcohol. I remember how we children would march in the streets, singing:

Ah! Don't drink that alcohol!
Ah! Don't even look at it!
Blessings for *Joseon society lie on her soberness!

*The name of Korea during its last royal dynasty (1392-1910)

돌아보니 대한기독교여자절제회에서 지어 교인들에게 퍼뜨린 노래였다. 우리는 어릴 때 이웃의 부모가 술을 마셔서 가산을 탕진하고 술로 고생하는 친구와 친지들을 보고 이 노래를 열심히 불렀다.

옛날 우리 집 앞에는 문전옥답이 있었다. 우리가 천진난만하게 뛰놀고 있을 때 가난한 아녀자들은 앞치마를 쥐고 이삭을 주웠다. 아버님은 일꾼들에게 벼를 모두 베어내지 못하게끔 명령하셨다.

"너희 땅의 곡물을 벨 때에

밭 모퉁이까지 다 베지 말며

떨어진 것을 줍지 말고

그것을 가난한 자와 거류민을 위하여 남겨두라.

나는 너희의 하나님 여호와니라."(레위기 23:22)

아버님은 이 말씀을 실천하셨다. 1920년대 한국은 아직 신분에 따른 차등이 심하였다. 함양 여(呂)씨라고 하면 양반의 가문이다. 아버님이 일찍 예수님을 믿지 않으셨다면 어머님의 선교 활동에 많은 지장이 있었을 것이다.

아버님은 평생 어머님과 함께 새벽기도에 꼭 참석하셨다.

Now I know that this song was composed and spread by the Korea Woman's Christian Temperance Union (KWCTU). When my brothers and I were young, our neighbors drank quite a bit of alcohol, causing much pain and suffering to their children and relatives, so we often sang this song to them.

There was a rice field in front of our house and, in the fall while we were innocently playing, poor women thrashed the rice and spread wide their aprons. My father instructed the workers to leave some of the harvest behind. For it is written:

> [22] *When you reap the harvest of your land,*
> *do not reap to the very edges of your field*
> *or gather the gleanings of your harvest.*
> *Leave them for the poor and the alien.*
> *I am the LORD your God.*
> *(Leviticus 23:22)*

My father put these words into practice. In the 1920s in Korea, the class system was still firmly enforced. My father was of the Yeu Clan of the Hamyang region—a respectable upper-class family. If my father hadn't come to Jesus early on, my mother would have faced many obstacles in her ministry, for she would have faced further oppression under

그런데 어느 추운 겨울, 하루는 아버님께서 철야예배에 다녀
오시는데 두루마기를 벗고 오셨다. 놀라서 묻는 우리에게 아
버님은 말씀도 하시지 않고 그냥 방으로 들어 가셨다. 나중에
알고 보니 오시는 길에 불쌍한 걸인이 떨고 있는 것을 보시고
벗어서 덮어주고 오셨다고 한다.

나는 외동딸로서 아버님의 사랑을 무척 많이 받고 자랐다.
1937년 4월 5일, 새벽 3시쯤 되니 아버님이 어머님께 "여보!
내가 6시 반이 되면 죽을 거요." 하셨다. 우리 온 식구는 5시
부터 모여 예배를 드렸다. 6시가 좀 지나니, 아버님은 두 손을
번쩍 드시며 말씀하셨다. "예수님이 나를 영접하러 오셔서 내
가 반가워서 손을 들었어요. '갈 길을 밝히 보이시니 주 앞에
빨리 나갑시다' 찬미를 불러줘요." 하셨다. 지금도 그때 아버
님이 기뻐하시던 모습이 눈에 선하다. 우리 온 가족은 함께 열
심히 찬송을 불렀다.

갈 길을 밝히 보이시니

1. 갈 길을 밝히 보이시니 주 앞에 빨리 나갑시다.
우리를 찾는 구주 예수 곧 오라 하시네.

the hierarchical class system.

Father went to early morning prayer meetings with my mother everyday. One cold winter day, my father returned home from church without his *durumagi*, a traditional Korean overcoat. Surprised, we asked him why he wasn't wearing his coat. Without a word, he went to his room. We later found out that on his way home, he saw a poor beggar shivering in the cold, so he took off his coat and covered the man with it.

As the only daughter, I was greatly loved by my father. At three o'clock in the morning on April 5, 1937, Father said to Mother, "Honey, I am going to die at 6:30 this morning." Our family gathered at five o'clock for worship. When it was a little past six, Father raised his two hands and said, "I'm raising my hands because I'm so glad to see Jesus coming to welcome me. Please sing the hymn 'Come to the Savior, Make No Delay'." I still vividly remember my father's joyous face. Our family sang the hymn with all our heart.

Come to the Savior, Make No Delay

1. Come to the Savior, make no delay;
   Here in His Word He has shown us the way;
   Here in our midst He's standing today,
   Tenderly saying, "Come!"

(후렴)

죄악 벗은 우리 영혼은 기뻐 뛰며 주를 보겠네.

하늘에 계신 주 예수를 영원히 섬기리.

2. 우리를 오라 하시는 말 기쁘게 듣고 즐겨하세.

구주를 믿기 지체 말고 속속히 나가세.

3. 주 오늘 여기 계시오니 다 와서 주의 말씀 듣세.

듣기도 하며 생각하니 참 이치시로다.

아버님이 운명하시니 시간은 6시 반이었다. 그 인자하시고 착하시던 성품을 다시 뵐 수 없게 되었다. 선교사님들이 보내 온 꽃다발은 청마루에 가득하였다.

(Refrain)
Joyful, joyful will the meeting be,
When from sin our hearts are pure and free;
And we shall gather, Savior, with Thee,
In our eternal home.

2. "Suffer the children!" Oh, hear His voice!
Let every heart leap forth and rejoice;
And let us freely make Him our choice;
Do not delay, but come.

3. Think once again, He is with us today;
Heed now His blest commands and obey;
Hear now His accents tenderly say,
"Will you, my children, come?"

When Father drew his last breath, it was exactly 6:30 a.m. And I never again beheld his graciousness and benevolence. Bouquets of flowers, sent by missionaries, filled the entire living room.

2. 나의 어린 시절

　내 나이 3세 때 우리 집에 벼락이 떨어져 온 식구가 화기를 먹고 내 머리맡에 놓였던 3층 장롱도 낙뢰에 가루가 된 일이 있었다. 그 틈에서 나는 방실방실 웃으며 머리털 하나도 다치지 않았다고 한다. 어머님은 그때 일을 이야기해 주시면서 "하나님께서 너를 이처럼 사랑하시니 부디 커서 주님이 기뻐하시는 일을 많이 해다오." 하고 늘 부탁하셨다.

　나는 5남 1녀 중 다섯째로 태어났다. 아들 넷을 낳고 딸을 기다리던 참이라 어머님 아버님뿐 아니라 온 교회가 기뻐했다. 내가 유년 시절에 많은 사랑을 받아왔기 때문에 그 사랑으로 남편과 자녀들 그리고 온 시댁 식구들을 나의 목숨보다 더 사랑했다. 또한 그 받은 사랑으로 지금도 미력하게나마 절제회를 사랑하며, 주님을 위하여 내 겨레를 위하여 거짓이 없는 사랑을 쏟고 있다.

　나는 13세 때에 이런 기도를 올린 기억이 난다. "인생에 있어서 한 번 죽는 것은 당연한 일인데, 약탕간을 머리에 두고 죽는 것보다 주님을 위해 순교하는 사람이 되게 해주시옵소서." 하나님께서는 이 기도를 응답하셔서, 매일매일을 순교자의 마음으로 살게 해주시니 이 은혜를 인하여 또한 감사드린다.

　부모에게 효성하는 사람이 나라에도 충성한다는 옛말처럼,

2. My Early Childhood

When I was three years old, our house was struck by lightning. Immediately afterwards, we heard a loud clap of thunder. My family felt the fiery heat caused by the lightning as a chest of drawers above me was struck and turned into dust. According to my mother, I was smiling beautifully in the midst of all the chaos. I had no injuries. Not a single strand of hair was ruffled. Mother said, "This is clearly a sign of God's incredible love for you my child. I urge you to dedicate your life to the Lord and to all that pleases Him."

I was the fifth child and the only daughter in a family of six children. After having four boys, my parents were eager to have a baby girl. Not only my parents but our entire church rejoiced when I was born.

I was able to love my husband, sometimes more than life itself, with the love I received during my childhood. And with the overflowing love I received, I loved my children and in-laws. And now I am able to love the KWCTU and pour out my most sincere love for Christ and this nation.

When I was only thirteen years old, I realized that we really only have one life to live. With this awakening, and moved by His grace, I prayed to God, "Dear Lord, may You bless me with the honor of dying a martyr for Jesus rather than dying of some illness." He has answered this prayer. I

나의 둘째 오빠는 애국 정신이 투철하였다. 일본 동지사대학 재학 당시, 대학의 어려운 공부를 하면서 일제의 교묘한 정치 선전에 맞서서 독립운동을 하는 것은 오빠에게 쉬운 일이 아니었다. 대학을 졸업하던 해에 어머님의 극진하신 간호에도 불구하고, 그렇게도 바라던 독립이 되기 3년 전에 그는 천국으로 갔다. 오빠는 나에게 "아가야! 우리 조선어 책을 모아두었다가 우리나라가 독립하거든 곧 내놓아라."라고 유언했다. 둘째 오빠는 현재 독립운동 기념관에 독립 유공자로 추대되어 있다.

live each day with the heart of a martyr. And for His grace, I am forever grateful.

It is said that anyone who is filial to one's parents is also loyal to one's country. This was true of my second eldest brother Kyu Hyung. He possessed a deep sense of patriotism. While he was attending Toshisha University in Japan, he campaigned with his school friends for the independence of Korea. But this was no easy task. Soon Kyu Hyung became ill from exhaustion. In spite of Mother's loving care, his illness progressed beyond treatment. He went to heaven the year of his graduation, just three years before Korea was liberated from Japanese colonial rule. Kyu Hyung made one last request to me: "Take care of all our Korean books," which were outlawed by Japanese authorities, "and as soon as Korea gains liberation, take them out and use them to educate the Korean people." Kyu Hyung is honored at the Korean Independence Hall for his dedication to this country.

3. 나의 여학교 시절

나는 대구에서 유일한 기독교 학교인 신명여고에 입학했다. 교장 선생님은 해리엇 폴라드(Harriet Pollard)라고 불리셨는데, 20대에 한국에 오셔서 60대까지 자기의 청춘을 전부 이 학교를 위해서 바치신 귀한 분이셨다. 용모도 아름답고 인품도 좋으셔서 신앙의 제자들을 얼마나 사랑하셨던지, 처녀 교장 선생님이셨는데 꼭 자기 친자식들같이 사랑하셨다.

우리는 미션 스쿨이라 아침 조회가 끝나면 항상 강당에 모여 예배를 드렸다. 나는 가정에서 늘 예배드리는 습관이 있어 이 채플시간이 가장 즐거운 시간이었다. 교장 선생님은 나를 무척 사랑하셨다. 교장 선생님께서 사회를 보시는 채플 시간에는 꼭 나에게 기도를 시키셨다.

교장 선생님이 중심이 되셔서 모이는 클럽이 있었는데, 성심회라는 학교의 가장 중심이 되는 클럽이었다. 고학년이 되어 이 클럽의 회장으로 뽑힌 나는 교장 선생님의 사랑을 더 많이 받게 되었다. 우리 학교에는 학교의 보물인 큰 성경책이 있었는데, 성심회를 졸업하는 회장이 그 책을 그 다음 회장에게 넘겨주는 것이 큰 행사였다.

내가 여학교 4학년이 되자 우리 학교 30주년 기념과 동시에 교장 선생님 회갑잔치가 있었다. 밤에는 대구에서 제일 큰

3. My High School Years

I went to Shin Myung Girls' High School, the only Christian school in Daegu at the time. The principal was Harriet Pollard. She was precious to us all. She came to Korea in her twenties and dedicated her life to the school until her retirement. Not only was she beautiful but also good-natured. Principal Pollard was single, but she loved her Christian students as though they were her own children.

Since our school was a Christian school, we had chapel every morning after our early morning meetings. Because I had always loved having family worship service at home, I enjoyed chapel above all my school subjects and activities. The principal loved me dearly and always asked me to pray at the school chapel service whenever she presided.

I was a member of a school club called the Sung Shim (sacred heart) Society, and our principal was its leader. When I was a senior, I was elected president of the club and was adored even more by Principal Pollard. We had a large Bible in our building. It was the school's greatest treasure. It was a school tradition for the graduating president to hand over this Bible to the next president of the Society.

In my senior year in high school, we celebrated both our school's 30th anniversary and also Principal Pollard's 60th birthday. We held a music concert at the largest community

공회당에서 음악회가 열렸다. 우리는 많은 노래 중에서 마지막에 헨델의 '메시야' 중 '할렐루야'를 불렀다. 우리 학교는 교육과 동시에 음악이 뛰어난 학교여서 대구에서는 우리 학교가 음악회를 개최하면 큰 인기였다.

centre in Daegu. We sang many songs and, at the end, we sang the Hallelujah Chorus from Handel's *Messiah*. Our school was well-known for its academic excellence as well as its excellence in music, so our concerts and performances were extremely popular in Daegu.

4. 나의 신학교 시절

내가 여학교 졸업반이 되니 교장 선생님께서 나에게 신학교에 가지 않겠느냐고 물으셨다. 나는 항상 순교하기를 원하던 참이라 너무나 기뻤다. 바로 "가겠습니다."라고 말씀 드렸더니 "모든 학비는 내가 부담하겠다."라고 하셨다. 나는 그 사랑에 크게 감격했다.

그때만 해도 여자 신학교는 한국에서 평양 한 곳밖에 없었다. 평양은 내가 대구에서 밤차를 타고 밤새도록 가면 11시간 반이 걸려서 아침 8시 반경에 도착하는 먼 곳이었다. 내 나이 17세 때였다. 첫 시간에 '소요리 문답'을 배웠다. 첫째 질문은 "인생의 제일 되는 목적이 무엇인가?"였다. 그 답은 "인생의 제일 되는 목적은 하나님을 영화롭게 하며, 영원토록 그를 즐겁게 하는 것이다."였다.

나는 이때 얼마나 큰 은혜를 받았던지! 내 생의 목표가 명확해지니 너무나 기뻤다. 신학교 시절에 소풍을 갔다. 대동강을 건너 멀리 모란봉을 바라보면서, 우리나라 교회 역사상 첫 순교자이신 토마스 목사님이 순교하신 그곳에 세워진 토마스 목사 순교 기념교회를 방문했던 그때의 감격은 무엇으로 표현할 것인가! 그 감격은 소풍이라기보다는 큰 부흥회에서 은

4. Pyeongyang Woman's Theological Seminary

When I was a senior in high school, Principal Pollard asked me if I would be interested in going to Pyeongyang Woman's Theological Seminary. I had always wanted to die a martyr, so I was glad to hear about this path that would bring me closer to that wish. I said yes immediately. To this she responded, "I will pay your tuition." I was deeply touched by her love.

At that time there was only one theological seminary for women in Korea and it was located in Pyeongyang. It took eleven and a half hours by train from Daegu to Pyeongyang. I was only seventeen years old at the time I attended my first lecture at seminary. It was at this lecture that I learned about the Westminster Confession of Faith. The first question that was asked was, "What is the foremost purpose of mankind?" The answer to that question is that man is made for the purpose of glorifying God and pleasing Him forever.

I was anointed by the Holy Spirit through that lecture! What a great joy it was for me to have the foremost purpose of my life clarified in such a way. One day, all the students at the seminary went on a picnic. I don't think I'll ever be able to express how deep my emotions were when I visited the memorial church for Reverend Robert J. Thomas, the first martyr in the history of the Protestant Church in Korea. A memorial church had been built on the very place he died for Jesus, a place that overlooks Moranbong above the Daedong

혜를 받고 돌아오는 기쁨과 같은 것이었다.

나는 어머님께 이런 편지를 썼다.

"어머님, 대구에서 어머님이 성경을 연구하시기 위해서 교회에 밤마다 가셨을 때는 제 나이가 어려 성경 말씀이 그다지 좋은 줄 미처 몰랐습니다. 제가 평양에 와서 성경을 본격적으로 공부를 하니 정말 어머님의 마음을 이해하겠습니다. 하나님 말씀이 이렇게 꿀 송이와 같이 단 줄 미처 몰랐습니다."

평양신학교에서 첫 학기를 마치고 여름방학에 집으로 돌아와, 교회 유년 주일학교에서 아이들을 가르치며 재미있는 방학을 마친 후 평양으로 올라갔다. 밤새 차를 타고 아침에 내려 학교에 가니 학교가 폐교되었다고 했다. 이유인즉 일본 사람들이 오만해져서 신사에 절하지 않는 학교는 문을 열지 못하게 한 것이다. 하도 어이가 없어 할 말도 잃고 있는데 졸업반 언니들은 지하실에 숨어서 수업을 하고 하급생들은 돌아가라는 지시였다. 우리는 모두 짐을 정리해서 돌아왔다. 길선주 목사님 같은 훌륭한 목사님들은 모두 옥에 갇히셨다. 순교의 바람이 세차게 불어왔다.

River. I was so moved and fully anointed by the Holy Spirit that I felt as though I had been to a revival meeting. I wrote the following letter to my mother:

After my first semester at seminary, I returned home for summer break, and with great joy I taught Sunday school at my home church. But after the break when I traveled hours by train and finally returned to school in Pyeongyang, I discovered that the school's doors had been sealed shut. The Japanese had forced the school to close. They had become very arrogant and had ordered all the schools that refused to bow before their gods to close. The younger students, dumbstruck by the news, were ordered to return home, while the seniors secretly studied in the basement of the school. The Japanese authorities arrested all who were seen talking to a missionary. Reverend Sun Joo Gil and many other respected ministers were thrown into prison. A harsh, violent wind blew, bringing forth many martyrs.

첫 순교자 토마스 목사님

대동강 언덕길을 조용히 올라가니
아담한 교회에는 아무도 있지 않네
우리는 감개무량해 무릎 꿇고 기도했네

주님을 위한 일은 헛되지 않더라고
무언의 교훈들이 성전에 가득 찼네
토마스 선교사님 순교 반열 계시지

그 옛날 목사님이 흘리신 순교의 피
오늘날 우리 겨레 영혼을 구원한
원동력 되었으므로 마음 깊이 감사해

순교한 그 모습을 내 아니 뵈었지만
돌로 맞아 피 흘리며 고요히 주님 앞에
기도로 무릎 꿇으시며 찬미하며 가셨지
주님! 우리 민족의 죄를 용서하여 주소서

(영국 웨일즈에서 오신 토마스 선교사님은 1866년 8월 30일 평양 대

Reverend Robert J. Thomas, the First Martyr

Climbing quietly up the hill near the Daedong River,
A small church stood empty.
Deeply moved, we knelt down in prayer.

Never in vain is our work for the Lord.
Unspoken instructions have filled the church.
Reverend Thomas, you now stand
with the ranks of martyrs.

The blood you shed as a martyr so long ago,
Became the driving force behind
the salvation of so many souls.
And for that, I am forever grateful.

Though I did not see you being martyred,
I know you were struck with stones and
bled quietly before the Lord.
Praying on your knees, you died praising the Lord.
O Lord! Forgive the sins of our nation.

(Reverend Robert J. Thomas, who was a Welsh missionary, arrived at the Daedong River on August 30, 1866, and was martyred by Mr. Chun Kwon Park on September 3, 1866. Mr. Chun Kwon Park became a Christian after reading the Bible

동강에 도착하여 9월 3일 박춘권에 의해 순교 당했다. 박춘권은 토마스 선교사님이 순교 시 주셨던 성경책을 읽고 그리스도를 믿게 되었다. 1907년 평양대부흥운동은 박춘권의 집에서 개척된 장대현교회에서 일어났다. 원산선교사수양회에서 하디 선교사님의 회개설교로 발단된 평양대부흥운동으로 은혜 받은 성도들은 고향에 돌아가 전도에 큰 힘을 썼고 이 무렵 나의 어머님 최성연 권사님도 전도 받으셨다.)

that Reverend Thomas gave him at the time of his martyrdom. In 1907, the Pyeongyang Revival took place at Changdaehyun Church, which was established at Mr. Chun Kwon Park's house. The Pyeongyang Revival, ignited by Canadian missionary R.A. Hardie's sermon on repentance, blessed many Christians who then returned to their hometowns and bore witness about Christ. During this period, Mrs. Sung Nyun Choi, my maternal grandmother, was led to Christ. Editor's note.)

5. 나의 신혼 시절

하나님을 위하여 순교하리라고 결심한 나는 아직 어려서 순교의 반열에 오르지 못하고 결혼을 하게 되었다. 혼처가 두 군데 들어왔다. 큰 부잣집에서 우리 신명학교 학생들 중에 제일 좋은 규수감을 구해달라고 학생처장인 이규원 선생님에게 부탁했다고 한다. 그는 나를 그 부잣집에 소개시키려고 했다. 어머님 대답이 "내가 딸이 둘이면 하나는 부잣집에, 하나는 인격을 보고 결혼시키겠는데, 단 하나밖에 없으니 인격을 보아야겠다." 하시면서 누차 권유하시는 것을 뿌리치셨다.

아버님이 돌아가신 후 하루는 어머님이 머리가 아파 쉬고 계시는데 어머님이 지도하시던 장년 주일학교 성경반 학생인 기묘임 씨(장래 시어머님이 되심)가 병문안을 오셨다. 평소에 교회에서 존경하는 선생님으로 어머님께 호감이 많던 그분은 어머님께 "형님 딸, 우리 며느리로 주세요."라고 하셨다. 그때 어머님은 주일학교 자신의 반에서 성경공부를 같이 하시는 분인 줄은 알았지만 가정 사정은 잘 모르는 상황에서 결혼 말씀을 하시니 웃으시며 "아직 너무 어립니다."라고만 대답히 셨다.

얼마 후 어머님이 그 댁을 지나시는데 동행했던 친구 분이 "이 댁이 기묘임 씨 댁입니다. 일부러라도 심방하실 댁이니 잠

5. Married Life

Although in my heart I was determined to die a martyr some day, I could not stand in the ranks of martyrs as I was too young. Two young men were likely candidates to become my husband. When a wealthy family asked Mr. Gyu Won Lee, who was dean of Shin Myung Girls' High School, to find their son a wife, Mr. Lee thought of me. Though he tried hard to convince my mother, she didn't agree to the idea and told him, "If I had two daughters, I would want one to get married to a rich man and the other to a very nice man, but since I only have one daughter, I'll find a good-natured man for her."

One day, after my father passed away, my mother was resting at home with a headache when Mrs. Myo Im Ki, who later became my mother-in-law and who was a part of the adult Bible study group my mother taught, paid Mother a visit. Mrs. Ki had tremendous respect for my mother and was very fond of her. Out of nowhere, she said to my mother, "I wish your daughter could become my daughter-in-law." My mother was very surprised to hear this because she knew Mrs. Ki only as one of her students and knew nothing of her family. Mother simply smiled and responded, "My daughter is still very young."

My mother and a friend of hers were passing Mrs. Ki's

시 들렀다가 가십시다.” 하고 권유했다. 어머님은 성경반 학생 댁이니 잠시 들어 가셨다. 그때 마침 저녁 무렵이라 그의 아들은 저녁을 들고 있었다. 기묘임 씨가 “얘야! 우리 선생님이시다. 인사드려라.” 하니, “네.” 하고 그 아들이 절을 하는데, 어머님께서 보시니 어찌나 좋은 인상인지 마음에 “내가 일생 기도하고 바라던 청년이 바로 이 사람이구나.”하시고 기뻐하셨다.

그 후 어머님은 목사님께 가셔서 이 일을 의논하시니 목사님이 “처음 믿으시는 가정이라 자세히는 모르겠지만, 그 청년의 방에는 항상 책이 가득 꽂혀있는 것으로 보아 독서를 많이 하는 모양입디다.”라고 말씀하셨다.

학벌을 알아보니 중학교 3학년을 마치고 중퇴하여 취직을 했다는 것이었다. 어머님은 큰 걱정이셨다. 그때는 여학교만 졸업했다고 하면 으레 신랑감은 전문학교나 대학생이라야 상대가 되었다. 그러나 어머님은 기도하시고 용단을 내리시고 큰오빠에게 의논하셨다. 그때 관서대학원 재학 중 여름방학에 나와 있던 큰오빠는 “어머님이 그렇게 마음에 드신다면 한번 봐야 하겠습니다. 저녁 때 그 사람에게 우리 집으로 오라고 전해주세요.”라고 대답했다.

저녁을 먹고 나서 나는 아래채에서 놀고 있었다. 대략 어

house one day. Her friend suggested that they stop by for a visit and, because Mrs. Ki was in Mother's Bible study class, Mother agreed to go in. It was early in the evening and Mrs. Ki's son, Soo Keun Kim, was eating dinner. Mrs. Ki said to her son, "Say hello. This is my Bible study teacher." He stood up promptly and bowed to my mother as he said hello. Deeply impressed by his good manners, my mother thought to herself, *This must be the young man I have been praying for and waiting for to become my son-in-law.*

My mother discussed her impressions of the young man with the pastor at our church. The pastor said, "I don't know much about Mrs. Ki or her family either as they are new to the church. One thing I know though is that Mrs. Ki's son reads a lot; there were many books in the young man's room."

Soo Keun had only attended junior high school and had left school in order to get a job. This worried my mother a great deal. In those days, there were few girls who graduated from high school—those who did usually married college or university graduates.

After days of prayer, Mother made up her mind and discussed the matter with my eldest brother Kyu Man, who was attending graduate school at Kansai University and who had just returned home for summer break. Kyu Man said: "If you are pleased with the young man, I would like to meet him. Please invite him to come over tonight."

머님께로부터 말씀은 들었다. 조금 있으니 아주 키가 큰 청년이 긴장된 얼굴로 우리 집 대문에 들어섰다. 나는 무의식 중에 그를 보고 방긋 웃었다. 그 후 그는 토로했다. 자기는 처남들이 다 대학생이라 해서 무척 긴장하고 들어 왔는데, 내가 웃어 주어서 얼마나 마음이 놓이고 고마웠는지 모른다고 말이다.

큰오빠는 그를 만났다. 밤이 자정이 되기까지 여러 가지를 묻기도 하고 이야기를 시키기도 했다. 밤이 늦어서 자기 집으로 돌아갔다. 큰오빠 대답이 "어머님! 학벌이 약하다 했는데, 이야기를 해 보니 대학교 졸업생보다 더 많은 독서를 했습니다." 하면서 별로 반대를 안 했다. 어머님은 크게 기뻐하셨다. 그러나 그 후 다른 오빠들과 교인들의 반대는 굉장했다. 그러나 어머님은 내게 이런 말씀을 하셨다. "아가야! 가마 밖의 천냥은 못 써도, 가마 안의 천냥은 쓴단다." 옛 속담인데, 돈이 많은 사람보다는 인격이 좋아야 된다는 뜻이었다.

어머님은 큰오빠가 나온 여름방학에 목사님을 모시고 약혼식을 올리게 했다. 양가의 어머님들은 기뻐하셨다. 약혼 후 그는 매일 우리 집에 놀러 왔다 그의 이야기에 의하면 자기 집은 옛날 큰 지주였는데, 유교를 믿으신 그 아버님께서 어찌나 효행이 지극하신지 할아버지가 돌아가시자 이불을 광목으로

After dinner, I was resting in the *araechae*—Korean houses usually have a main area, the *keunchae*, which is the parents' space, and another area called the *araechae*, which is where the guest and children's rooms are located—when my mother told me that Soo Keun would visit us that night. A little while later, a tall young man with a tense expression on his face entered through the front gate. Upon seeing him, I unknowingly smiled at him. Soo Keun later confessed that he was nervous about meeting my brothers, who were all university graduates, but that he instantly felt relaxed upon seeing me smile that night.

Kyu Man asked Soo Keun many questions about various subjects, and the two talked until midnight. After Soo Keun left our house, my brother gave Mother his opinion. "You told me he received little education, but the young man has read more books than most university graduates." Kyu Man didn't seem to object to the idea of me getting engaged to the man. Mother was pleased to hear of his approval. On the other hand, all my other brothers and the church members strongly objected to the marriage. Mother told me an old Korean proverb: "A wagon carrying a thousand *nyang*—old unit of Korean money—on the outside is useless, but a wagon carrying a thousand *nyang* inside is very useful." She wanted me to understand that good character was much more valuable and important than wealth in a man.

만들고 요는 짚으로 만들고 삼베로 만든 상복을 세 벌이나 떨어지도록 입으셨고, 삼 년 후 그의 아버님도 몸이 약하여져서 결국 세상을 떠나셨다. 그때 그는 아직 10세밖에 안 되었는데, 집안에 형님이 한 분 계셨으나 술과 기생으로 몇 년 안에 그 많은 재산을 다 탕진했다고 한다. 그래서 그가 어릴 때부터 신문 배달을 해야만 학교에 갈 수 있을 정도로 가세가 기울어졌다. 그 당시 대구상업중학교라고 하면 수재만 뽑을 때였는데, 그는 입학은 했지만 학비의 조달이 어려워서 중퇴하고 말았다. 그 후 그는 일본 사람이 경영하는 삼국상회라는 회사에 취직을 했다.

그의 어머님에 의하면 그는 부잣집 선비 가정에 태어나서 어릴 때 어찌나 머리가 영특한지, 4세 때 천자문과 동문서책을 모두 뗄 정도로 수재였다고 한다. 그 아버님이 귀여워서 항상 사랑방에서 아버님 옆에 두시고 글을 읽게 하시고 붓글씨를 가르치시며 귀하게 키우셨다. 한번은 문호당이라는 선비가 글 짓는 곳에 데리고 가셨다가 꽃 한 송이를 끊어 주셨는데, 이 꽃을 집에 가지고 와서 꽃병에 꽂아 놓고 붓글씨를 쓰다가 잠이 들었다. 그때 그 아버님이 오셔서 붓글씨 써 놓은 솜씨를 보시고, "나는 어릴 때 이렇게 못 썼는데……." 하시면서 기뻐하시는 것을 그가 잠결에 들었다고 한다.

Our engagement ceremony was held in the summer when Kyu Man returned for summer break. My mother and Mrs. Ki were very happy. Soo Keun came to our house every day thereafter. I found out that Soo Keun's father was a rich landlord and a devoted Confucian who had mourned his father's death by sleeping on a straw mattress with a blanket made out of rough cotton cloth and by wearing garments made of hemp. In the process of mourning his father's death, Soo Keun's father wore out three sets of hemp clothes. Three years later when my fiancé was only ten years old, his father became very ill and passed away. From early childhood, Soo Keun earned money for tuition as a newspaper boy. Although he was accepted to the prestigious Daegu Commercial High School, he had to withdraw when he was halfway done because he could no longer afford the tuition. He got a job afterwards at Samguk Co., Ltd., which was then owned and operated by the Japanese.

My mother-in-law told us that there had been many scholars in the family tree and that her son, inheriting that particular trait, had shown signs of bright intelligence since early childhood. According to her, he was so smart that he mastered a primer of Chinese characters, *The Thousand-Character Classic*, and also the next level, the *Dongmong Seonseup*, when he was just three years old. His father was very fond of him and always had him nearby, and with much care and love, taught him how to read and how to write with a calligraphy brush. My husband told me that his father once took him to a *mun ho dang*, a place where

　그 후 머리는 수재인데 공부를 중단해서 그는 마음이 괴로웠다. 삼국상회에서 좀 떨어진 곳에 '칠성교회'가 있었다. 아무도 그에게 전도하지 않았으나, 하나님의 부르심을 받아 그 교회에 새벽예배를 3개월 동안 다녔다. 그때 그는 하나님께 "하나님! 저에게 정직한 사람이 되게 하시고 큰 일을 할 수 있게 해 주옵소서!"하고 기도를 드렸다. 훗날 그는 이 칠성동 일대에서 큰 회사의 기반을 잡고 성공하게 되었다. 새벽기도에 참석하고 얼마 후 그는 어머님께 "어머님! 혼자 계시니 심심하신데, 예수님을 믿으세요." 하고 전도했다. 귀한 아들의 권유라 그 어머님은 교회에 나오셨다가, 우리 어머님이 가르치시던 장년 여자 성경반의 학생이 되셨다.

　나의 어머님은 새벽기도도 안 빠지시지만, 낮에도 항상 성경학교 강당에 올라가셔서 하나님께 기도를 드리셨다. 하루는 성경학교 강당에서 기도를 드리시는데, "사위 공부 보내라." 하시는 음성이 들렸다. 어머님이 눈을 떠보시니 아무도 없었다. "내가 사람됨만을 보고 딸을 약혼시켰더니 아무래도 내 마음의 소리인가 보다." 하고 장소를 옮겨서 또 기도를 드리셨다. 다시 "사위 공부 보내라." 하시는 음성이 들렸다. 그제서야 하나님의 음성이심을 깨닫고 어머님은 기쁘게 집으로 돌아오셨다.

scholars gathered and wrote poems. There his father picked a flower and gave it to him. Soo Keun brought it home and placed it in a vase. He then went to his room to practice calligraphy for a while before he fell asleep. When his father came home, Soo Keun overheard his father joyfully say, "I couldn't write this well when I was his age."

Soo Keun had a genuine love and interest for learning, and he was very sad when he couldn't continue his studies. There was a church called Chilsung Presbyterian Church located near his workplace. Though he had never heard the Gospel, led by the Holy Spirit, he attended early morning services at that church for three months. He prayed, "God! May I live an honest life and do great works!" He eventually started his own business in the same district. I believe that the Lord God Almighty listened to his prayers. Soo Keun even convinced his mother to believe in God. "Dearest mother, believe in Jesus and you won't be lonely anymore." Through her son's witnessing, she started attending church and later joined an adult Bible class, the very one my mother taught.

My mother attended the early morning service at church every day. She also used to go to the auditorium at the Bible school to pray during the day. While praying one day in the auditorium, she heard a clear voice tell her, "Send your son-in-law abroad to study." My mother looked around to see who had spoken to her, but no one was around her. She thought, *It must be the voice of my conscience that is troubled over having allowed my only daughter to get engaged to a man with little education, simply for his character.* So she moved to another

그날 밤 그가 우리 집에 놀러 오자 어머님은, "이 사람아! 공부하러 가면 어떻겠나?" 하고 물으셨다. 그는 바로 "네, 가겠습니다." 하고 대답했다. 그는 7년 동안 벌어놓은 3,000원을 가지고 동경으로 가서 일본 대학에 입학을 하고 밤에는 중학 과정, 낮에는 대학 과정을 공부했다. 그는 3년 동안 매우 열심히 공부를 하여 3년 만에 두 과정을 마쳤는데, 일본 대학에서는 3,000명 졸업생 중에서 최우수상을 받았다.

그가 유학할 당시 동경에는 전쟁의 여파로 물자가 부족해서, 그는 영양 부족으로 폐결핵에 걸렸다. 당시 항생제가 없어서 폐결핵에 걸리면 사형선고와 다름없었기에 어머님은 나를 보면 눈물이 나서 앞을 못 보셨다. 그러나 어머님은 내게 "아가야! 우리가 하나님 앞에서 한 언약인데, 어찌 몸이 약하다 해서 거절하겠니? 그러니까 가서 아들 하나만 낳아라. 그러면 너는 삶에 큰 보람이 있을 거야." 하셨다.

그가 졸업반 되던 해 1941년 10월 27일, 우리는 결혼했다. 참으로 맑은 날이었다. 3일 만에 시댁에 가는데 내 마음은 한없이 무거웠다. 우리 집은 모두 신앙의 가정이지만, 시댁은 어머님이 겨우 어린아이 같은 신앙이이시고 온 문중은 예수님을 몰랐다. 삼촌댁들은 예수 믿는 사람을 미워하였다. 나는 시집가는 날 이렇게 기도드렸다.

spot to pray. She again heard the same voice say, "Send your son-in-law to study abroad." She then realized that it was God's voice and returned home joyfully.

That night when Soo Keun came to our house to see me, my mother asked, "Dear, would you like to study abroad?" He immediately answered, "Yes, I would love to." He went to Tokyo with 3,000 won, which was everything he had saved for seven years, and was admitted to Nihon University. During the day he studied at the university, and at night he attended high school. Studying hard, he was able to complete both schools in three years. He graduated university with the top grades among 3,000 students.

There wasn't enough food in Tokyo when he studied there, because Japan had started the Pacific War. Soo Keun eventually contracted tuberculosis due to malnutrition. My mother became very concerned upon hearing the news, especially since tuberculosis signified death, for antibiotics were nearly nonexistent those days. My mother could not bear to look at me, for tears filled her eyes. She said to me, "My dear child, you got engaged in the presence of the Lord; how then could we dare to break the promise we made before God because of Soo Keun's sickness? May you at least give birth to a baby boy; I promise you, you will then understand that life really is worth living."

My fiancé and I got married on October 27, 1941, the year he graduated. It was a very clear day. Three days after the wedding ceremony, I moved into his house with a very heavy heart. Only my mother-in-law believed in Christ, and she was

　"하나님 아버지! 저는 요셉이 보디발의 집에 팔려 가는 것과 같은 외로운 심정입니다. 시댁 식구들이 거의 예수님을 모르니, 요셉과 함께 하신 하나님 저와 함께 하여 주시옵소서. 예수님 이름으로 기도합니다. 아—멘."

　인격 하나만 보고 간 시댁은 가난하였다. 방이 셋 있었는데 방 하나는 남에게 세를 주고 방 두 개만 쓰고 있었다. 어찌나 집이 낮은지 나는 방에 들어갈 때마다 큰 고역이었다. 며칠이 지나니 남편은 동경으로 갔다. 아직 유학 중이었고 시어머님은 병환 중이셔서 우리는 신혼여행도 못 갔다. 날은 몹시도 추웠고 매일 고된 일들로 하루하루를 보내야 했다. 병환으로 계신 시어머니의 대소변도 받아야 했다. 나는 이 가문에 그리스도의 사랑을 전하러 온 사명감을 가지고 열심히 일하며 어머님을 섬겼다. 어머님은 내가 대소변을 비울 때 전혀 냄새가 안 나는 듯 태연히 웃으며 치우니, 처음에는 가식인줄 알고 문구멍으로 내다보았다고 하셨다. 그러나 어머님 앞에서와 우물가에서 하는 나의 태도가 동일하니, 그제서야 '저 며느리가 마음이 착하구나.' 하고 감동하셨다고 한다. 지금도 생각하면 신기한 것은 지성으로 섬기니 한 번도 냄새가 나지 않았다는 것이다.

still quite young spiritually. The rest of Soo Keun's household did not know Christ at all. In fact, Soo Keun's uncles hated Christians and referred to them as "Jesus freaks." I offered this prayer to God the day after my wedding:

<blockquote>
Heavenly Father!
I feel as alone as Joseph felt when he was sold to
Potiphar's house. My in-laws do not know You.
May You, the God who walked with Joseph, now
walk with me. In Jesus Christ's name I pray. Amen.
</blockquote>

I married my husband only considering his character. My in-laws were very poor. They owned a three-room house, but having rented one room out to a tenant, they had use of only two of the rooms. I had trouble standing erect in my room because the ceiling was so low.

Soo Keun went back to Tokyo a few days later. Since he still had not completed his studies and because his mother was ill, we could not go on our honeymoon. As the days became colder, the everyday household chores became more demanding. Soon, my mother-in-law became bedridden and I was responsible for helping her use a bedpan. Since I wanted to share the love of Christ with my in-laws, I faithfully looked after my mother-in-law. Because I always smiled whenever I changed her bedpan, she thought I was only pretending and covering up my resentment toward her. Whenever I left the room to clean the bedpan, she would look

그 후 어머님의 병환은 점점 더 위중하셨다. 나는 너무 걱정이 되어서 동경에 전보를 쳤다. 남편은 그때 마침 중요한 시험 직전이었다. 전보를 받고 그는 생각했다. 시험은 내년에 또 있지만 어머님이 세상을 떠나시는데 뵈러 가지 않으면 불효가 된다고 생각하고 그는 한국으로 돌아왔다. 병원에 입원을 하시고 치료한 결과 좀 차도가 있었다. 곧 그는 동경으로 다시 돌아갔다. 그때 나는 태기가 있었다. 나는 친정 어머님으로부터 일찍 태교에 대해서 배웠다. 그래서 성경만 봉독하고 다른 서적은 일체 보지 않았다. 멀리서 싸움 소리가 나면 귀를 닫았고, 귀중한 생명이 아름다운 인격으로 태어나도록 하나님께 열심히 기도드렸다.

가난하고 고달픈 시집살이지만 성령의 충만한 기쁨으로 매일을 지냈다. 부엌에서 불을 땔 때에는 "하나님 아버지! 저의 죄를 불과 같이 태워 주소서." 그릇을 씻을 때에는 "하나님 아버지! 저의 죄를 물과 같이 말갛게 씻겨 주소서." 하고 기도드리며 감사하며 지냈다. 내 가슴에는 하나님의 사랑과 기쁨이 매일 우물같이 솟아났다. 빨리 빨래와 청소를 하고는 어머님 방에 가서 찬송을 부르고 예배를 드리며 위로해 드렸다, 시어머님은 항상 나의 찬양 소리를 기뻐하셨다.

영대의 출산 예정일은 1942년 10월 2일이었다. 아침에 배

out the window to see whether I was still smiling. Seeing how my attitude didn't change, she told others that she was very impressed by my kindness. It still amazes me when I think back to how I didn't smell anything bad when I changed my mother-in-law's bedpan.

My mother-in-law became more ill as the days passed, so I sent a telegram to Tokyo. Soo Keun, upon receiving the news, immediately came back home. He said he could always take the bar exam the following year, but if his mother were to pass away, he would never be able to see her again and he would be an unworthy son. After being hospitalized, my mother-in-law's condition improved a great deal. Soon after my husband went back to Tokyo to continue his studies, I realized that I was pregnant. I had learned about the importance of special prenatal care from my mother, so I only read the Bible, never secular books. If I heard people arguing nearby, I plugged my ears. I diligently prayed to God that he would give me a child with a beautiful character.

Though I had a lot of work to do and lived in poverty, I lived with joy each day, fully anointed by the Holy Spirit. Whenever I made a fire for the kitchen stove, I prayed, "Heavenly Father, burn away all my sins in a blazing fire like the one before me." Whenever I washed the dishes, I prayed, "Heavenly Father, wash away all my sins just as water washes the residue off these dishes." The joy and love of the Lord sprang out of my heart every day like water from a fountain. After I finished doing the laundry and cleaning the house, I would go to my mother-in-law's room and comfort

가 살살 아팠다. 시어머님이 편찮으시니 친정에 갈 수도 없는 사정이어서 친정에 통지를 했더니 어머님이 오셨다. 그 착하신 나의 어머님은 시어머님 병간호와 딸의 해산과 몸조리까지 열심히 도와주시고 영대 백일이 지나셔야 집으로 돌아가셨다.

하루는 시어머님이 나를 부르셨다. "아가야! 내가 예수님을 믿고 이 병이 들었다. 동서들은 예수 안 믿는데 다 건강하지 않니? 내가 죽어도 원이 없게 무당을 불러서 굿을 한번 해다오." 하셨다. 나는 이것이 잠깐 찾아온 마귀의 시험임을 즉시 깨달았다. 내 방에 와서 하나님께 기도를 드렸다. "하나님 아버지! 능력을 베푸셔서 우리 시어머님을 찾아온 마귀를 물리쳐 주시옵소서. 주님의 큰 영광을 보게 해주시옵소서. 예수님의 이름으로 기도드립니다. 아-멘." 하고 기도드렸다. 잠시 후 나는 시어머님이 계시는 큰방에 가서, "어머님! 어머님이 만약 굿을 해서 낫는다 치더라도, 이 세상에는 20년 아니면 30년밖에 더 살 수 없습니다. 그러나 하나님의 세계는 영원합니다. 어머님, 이 짧은 세월과 영원, 둘 중에 어느 것을 택하시겠습니까?" 하고 말씀드렸다. 바로 그때 마귀는 물러가고 시어머님은 회개하셨다. "아가야! 잘못했다. 내가 하도 아프니까 그만 마음이 약해져서 그러니 목사님을 모셔다가 기도를 받자."

her by singing hymns and worshipping God with her. She always seemed to enjoy the sound of my voice singing songs of praise.

My first baby was expected on October 2, 1942. On that morning, the pain in my belly grew sharper and sharper. I couldn't go to my mother's house because my mother-in-law was so ill. So I sent Mother a telegram and she came over. My godly mother earnestly took care of not only me after I gave birth but also my bed-ridden mother-in-law. And only after my baby boy Young Tae turned 100 days old did Mother return home.

My mother-in-law once said: "I got sick when I started believing in Jesus. Why are my sisters-in-law all healthy when they are not Christians? Please send for an exorcist so that after death my spirit won't regret not having tried that method." I was too shocked to say a word. I immediately realized that this was a temptation from Satan. I went to my room and prayed to God. "Heavenly Father, I ask that You drive away the evil spirits that have a hold on my mother-in-law. May we experience Your great glory. In Jesus' name I pray. Amen." Afterwards, I went over to my mother-in-law's room and told her: "Mother, let's say you get well through an exorcism and live another twenty or thirty years, but you know God's world lasts an eternity. Which will you choose? Twenty to thirty more years in this world? Or an eternal life with God?" With these words, Satan left her and she repented. "I am sorry my child. I have sinned. I allowed my weakening body to weaken my heart. Please call the pastor and ask him

그래서 나는 달려가 목사님을 모셔 왔다. 친정 어머님도 오시게 했다. 그때 주신 성경 말씀이 마태복음 26장 30절 '이에 그들이 찬미하고 감람산으로 나아가니라.' 이었다. 예수님께서 십자가를 앞에 두시고도 찬미하셨다는 말씀에 어머님은 큰 은혜를 받고 회개의 눈물을 흘리시며 거듭나셨다. 이제 어머님의 마음은 천국으로 변하셨다.

음력 정월 삼일, 주일이었다. 아무래도 어머님 중세가 위독해 보였다. 그래서 나는 교회에 가지 않고 빨리 설거지를 끝내고 어머님과 주일예배를 드렸다. 먼저 나는 '저 요단강 건너편에'를 불러드렸더니 어머님은 기쁨으로 충만해지셨다.

"저 요단강 건너편에 화려하게 뵈는 집 주
날 위해 예비하신 집일세.
그 강가에 생명 나무 꽃이 만발하였네.
주의 낯을 그 곳에서 뵈오리."
(찬송가 224장)

그 찬송을 부르고 나니 한 곡을 더 부르라고 하셨다. 그래서 '주가 맡긴 모든 역사'를 불렀다.

to come and pray for me."

I ran to get the pastor and asked my mother to come as well. We read a passage from the Bible: "When they had sung a hymn, they went out to the Mount of Olives." (Matthew 26:30) My mother-in-law was greatly moved by the Word of God. She was renewed by the Holy Spirit and tearfully repented of her sins as she realized that Christ had given praise even though He had yet to bear His cross. My mother-in-law's heart began to change as she began to fix her eyes on heaven.

The third day of the Lunar New Year was a Sunday. My mother-in-law's condition became so critical that I couldn't even go to church. I quickly finished washing the dishes and had a time of worship with her. She was filled with joy when I sang the first verse of Hymn 224:

Face to Face with Christ, My Savior

Face to face with Christ, my Savior,
Face to face—what will it be,
When with rapture I behold Him,
Jesus Christ who died for me?

Then she asked me to sing one more hymn, so I sang Hymn 231:

"주가 맡긴 모든 역사 힘을 다해 마치고
밝고 밝은 그 아침을 당할 때
요단강을 건너가서 주의 손을 붙잡고
기쁨으로 주의 얼굴 뵈오리
나의 주를 나의 주를 내가 그의 곁에 서서 뵈오며
나의 주를 나의 주를 손에 못자국을 보아 알겠네."
(찬송가 231장)

그 마지막 절에 "세상 고생 모두 잊어버리리" 찬양을 부른 후, "어머님, 지금 고생은 하나님 앞에 가시면 꿈과 같이 잊게 된답니다."하고 위로를 해드렸더니, 기뻐하시며 기도하시자고 하여 내가 기도를 했다. 어머님은 기도하시는 중에 소천하셨다. 너무도 행복한 임종을 허락하신 주님께 감사를 드렸다. 교인들과 함께 드린 엄숙한 장례식은 믿지 않던 집안 어른들께 많은 전도가 되었다.

When My Life Work is Ended

When my life work is ended
and I cross the swelling tide,
When the bright and glorious morning I shall see,
I shall know my Redeemer
when I reach the other side,
And his smile will be the first to welcome me.

After I sang the last verse, I comforted my mother-in-law. "Mother, when we go to heaven, all the sufferings we endured in this world will be forgotten as though they were but a dream." She nodded in agreement and we knelt down together to pray. At the end of my prayer, I didn't hear her say *Amen*. She left for heaven while praying. What a blessing! I thanked the Lord. My mother-in-law's funeral was a blessed time of witnessing Jesus Christ to many relatives.

6. 나의 첫 시골 생활

시어머님이 병중이실 때 남편은 금융조합 이사 시험에 수석 합격하여 어머님의 마음을 크게 기쁘게 해드렸다. 그로 인해 우리는 남편의 부임지로 가야 했는데, 큰 시동생을 혼자 두고 갈 수가 없었다. 그래서 그를 결혼하게 돕고 집과 논밭을 모두 큰 시동생에게 주고, 단출한 모습으로 우리는 경북 영주의 부임지에 찾아갔다.

영주 금융조합 부이사 사택은 참 훌륭했다. 마당에 토마토도 심고 채소도 가꾸니 도시에서만 살았던 나는 매우 즐거웠다. 4개월의 연수 후 남편은 실령 금융조합으로 발령이 나서 우리 가족은 실령으로 갔다. 그곳에는 전기가 없어서 등을 켜야 했다. 사택 마당에는 마침 초가을이라 청포도가 주렁주렁 열려 있었다. 뒤뜰에는 부지런한 전임 이사님이 가꾼 호박, 오이, 부추, 상추, 토마토, 가지, 고추 등 일용할 채소들이 잘 자라고 있었다. 우리는 하나님께 감사를 드렸다.

그때는 일제 말엽이라서 나는 교회 갈 때에도 시장바구니에 성경을 담아야만 갈 수 있었다. 실령의 교회는 자그마했다. 권 목사님이 계셨는데, 그 댁 자부가 대구의 한 교회 교인으로 친구였다. 목사님 내외분이 훌륭하셔서 은혜로웠다. 나는 교회 외에는 아무 데도 출입을 하지 않았다.

6. Our Life in the Countryside

When my mother-in-law was still living, Soo Keun took an examination for bankers and passed with the top score. This pleased her greatly. I was supposed to move to where Soo Keun was appointed assistant director of a Farmers Bank. But this meant leaving my younger brother-in-law all by himself. When a wedding date was set for him, Soo Keun and I gave him our house and the rice field. With my son on my back and my husband next to me, the three of us moved to Yeongju.

Soo Keun had to spend some time in Yeongju as an assistant director for his apprenticeship. The house that was provided for us was very big. I grew tomatoes and various kinds of vegetables in the garden. I was truly happy there, away from city life. After the four-month apprenticeship, Soo Keun was appointed director of the Farmers' Bank in Sillyeong, so we moved again. There was no electricity in Sillyeong. We had to use kerosene lamps. At the house that was provided for us, sweet green grapes hung in clusters on their vines. The former director had grown various kinds of vegetables, including pumpkins, cucumbers, leeks, lettuce, tomatoes, eggplants, and green hot peppers in the backyard. We thanked God for the wonderful house.

While we were living in Sillyeong, Japanese oppression was nearing its end, but even then, I had to hide my Bible in a shopping basket whenever I went to church. The church in

　이곳에 3년을 거주하는 동안 우리는 1945년 6월 23일, 둘째 아들 영민이를 낳았다. 남편은 가난한 우리 농민들을 돕기 위해 헌신적으로 일하였다.

Sillyeong was a small community church. A Reverend Kwon, whose daughter-in-law was a friend of mine from my home church in Daegu, was ministering there. The reverend and his wife were such wonderful people that the church was always filled with God's grace.

During our three-year stay in Sillyeong, our second son Young Min was born on June 23, 1945. Seeing the miserable conditions that the farmers lived in, Soo Keun felt compassion for them and worked hard to improve their status and living conditions.

7. 8·15 해방

1945년 8·15 해방의 소식이 들렸다. 우리는 너무나 기뻐서 무엇이라고 표현하기 어려웠다. 그저 하나님께 감사를 드릴 뿐이었다. 일본 정부는 물러가고 아직 한국 정부는 서지 않았으니, 해방의 기쁨과 동시에 큰 혼란이 일어났다. 이때까지 입이 있어도 말 못하던 우리 민족의 울분이 터져 나왔다. 이제까지 일본인 앞잡이가 되어 있던 면장을 죽인다고 사람들은 이곳 저곳을 찾아 다니고 일본 사람들은 숨죽이며 달아나고 말았다. 그때 우리 집에는 시골 분들이 소고기를 많이 가지고 왔다. 나는 깜짝 놀랐다. 워낙 뇌물을 싫어하는 남편이라서 이유를 물어 보았더니, 그분들 대답이 "이것은 뇌물이 아닙니다. 해방이 되어 우리 동네에서 경사를 축하하여 소를 한 마리 잡았는데, 이제 이사님 은혜에 감사드리려고 가져온 것입니다. 거절하시면 안됩니다."하고 말했다. 우리는 무척 감격스러웠다.

남편은 다시 영천으로 발령이 났다. 해방 후 인플레가 대단했다. 다행히도 그 곳에는 전기가 있었다. 우리는 실령에 있을 동안 열심히 저축했다. 3년 동안 3,000원이라는 큰 돈을 모았다. 쌀 배급과 십일조 외에는 돈을 쓰지 않았다. 그러나 해방이 되니 영천에 와서 3개월 만에 모두 지출하게 되었다. 이제

7. The August 15th Liberation

We heard the news that Korea was liberated on August 15, 1945. The joy we felt was so great that no amount of words can fully describe it. We thanked and praised God again and again. The Japanese government was being expelled but the Korean government had not yet been established; along with the joy of liberation came chaos. The rage of the oppressed Koreans, who had not been able to speak out for fear of punishment, suddenly exploded. People tried to hunt down the Korean magistrates that had sided with the Japanese. The Japanese living in Korea fled out of fear. To my surprise, the people in our town brought a large amount of beef to us one day. Since my husband hated bribes of any kind, I had to ask them why they had brought us the meat. They explained: "This is not a bribe. We've always been grateful for Soo Keun's kindness. We figured we've already butchered this meat to celebrate the liberation of our country; the least we can do is share it with him. Please don't refuse. This is a token of our gratitude." Soo Keun and I were deeply touched by their sincere hearts.

Soo Keun was reappointed director and was relocated to the Farmers' Bank in Yeongcheon. There was electricity in Yeongcheon. While we were in Sillyeong, we were able to save money—in three years, we had managed to save 3,000 won, which was quite a large amount of money then. We didn't spend any of Soo Keun's earnings, except on tithing and

금융조합 이사 월급만으로는 도저히 가계를 꾸려 나갈 수 없는 지경이 되었다. 그때 우리는 막내 시동생 장가도 들여야 되고, 일본에서 돌아온 시누님 식구도 우리 보호만 기대하고 있었다.

남편이 일을 잘 처리하니, 그때 상주 금융조합에서 폭동이 일어나서 "유능한 이사를 보내야 되겠다." 하고는 전근 온 지 3개월 만에 상주로 또 전근 명령을 내렸다. 남편은 이 시기를 타서 사표를 냈으나 반려되었다. 그러나 다시 사표를 내고 사정을 설명한 끝에 수리되었다. 우리는 만 3년이 안 됐으므로 퇴직금도 못 타서 이사할 돈이 없었다. 남편은 대구에 가서 친구에게 돈을 5,000원 빌려 트럭을 한 대 구해와서 이사를 했다.

금융조합 동지들이 조합의 돈을 융자해주어 대봉동에 위치한 집을 사게 되어 매우 기뻤다. 1948년 2월 17일, 큰딸 영주가 태어났다. 아들 둘 다음이라서 어찌나 귀여운지 "어머님이 나를 놓고 이렇게 기뻐하셨겠지……." 하고 회상했다.

buying rice. After liberation, we spent all our savings within three months after moving to Yeongcheon because of the high inflation rate. We had a lot to worry about because it was getting harder to get by on my husband's salary alone. Not only was my husband's youngest brother getting married, but his sister was returning from Japan with her husband, three daughters, and three sons, having heard the joyful news of liberation. They were expecting to receive some financial support from us.

Soo Keun was transferred to Sangju just three months after our move to Yeongcheon. He gladly took the offer as an opportune time for him to submit his resignation, but it wasn't processed. He handed in his resignation once again, explaining our situation. Only then did the board members reluctantly accept his resignation. My husband was not eligible for severance pay because he had worked at the bank for only three years. We didn't have enough money to move, so Soo Keun borrowed 5,000 won from a friend to rent a moving truck, and we moved back to Daegu.

His banker friends helped us get a loan from a bank to buy a house in Daebong-dong. We were very happy. On February 17, 1948, our third child and first daughter, Young Joo, was born. To me she seemed quite cute, and a truly wonderful, indescribable feeling that I hadn't felt with the birth of my two sons filled my heart. I thought, *Mother must have felt this happy when she held me, her only daughter, in her arms.*

8. 나의 중생

　나는 23세 때 집사가 되었다. 어머님이 권사가 되신 그 해였다. 영주를 낳고 젖을 먹이던 중 하루는 교회에 가서 요한일서 1:10 말씀에 큰 감동이 되었다.

“만일 우리가 범죄하지 아니하였다 하면

하나님을 거짓말 하는 이로 만드는 것이니

또한 그의 말씀이 우리 속에 있지 아니하니라.”

(요한일서 1:10)

　나는 성령으로 충만하신 어머님께 태교를 받고 태어났고 신학교도 다녔던 터라 별로 죄지은 생각이 나지 않았다. 그러나 인간은 다 죄가 있다고 하니, 하나님께 간절히 기도해 봐야겠다고 생각하고 3일 동안 금식하기로 했다. 하루 반을 금식을 하던 중 마치 방안의 바닥을 닦으면 깨끗해 보이지만 햇볕이 들어오면 수 많은 먼지가 훤히 보이듯이 하나님께 지은 죄 17가지가 나왔다. 목사님께 자복하려니까, 찬양대원이요 교회 집사인데 정말 부끄러운 마음이 들었다. 죄는 자복해야만 하니 우리 주 예수께 모두 자복하고 많이 통회했다.

　그 후 하늘에서 큰 기쁨이 내렸다. 가리우는 것이 없는 경

8. Born Again

I was only twenty-three years old at the time when I was nominated deaconess. My mother became an elderwoman that very same year. One day at church while feeding Young Joo, I was convicted by the Holy Spirit while meditating upon 1 John 1:10.

I was filled with the Holy Spirit at birth, thanks to the prayers my mother prayed while I was still in her womb. And having attended a theological seminary as a youth, I didn't think much about the sin in me. The passage clearly declared that all men are sinners, so I prayed to God. I decided to go on a three-day fast. After a day and a half, God revealed roughly seventeen sins that I had committed but hadn't realized before. I thought my heart was like a room that had been swept clean. But in fact, it was a room with a layer of dust that, revealed by sunlight, had settled thinly on the surface of my heart. I wanted to go see the pastor, but I was too ashamed, for I was a deaconess and member of the

지에 이르니 하늘의 기쁨이 마음에 차고 넘쳤다. 나는 항상 주님께 상의를 드리고 일을 시작하게 되었다. 길을 걸어도 일을 해도 기뻤다. 고기가 얕은 물에서 놀다가 깊은 바다에 들어간 것처럼 하나님이 주시는 무한한 기쁨을 누리게 된 것이다.

church choir. However, a pressing need to repent could no longer be tamed, so I repented of my sins and confessed them to our Lord Jesus.

A great sense of joy from heaven swept over me afterwards. Since I was freed from my sins, the joy of heaven overflowed in me. Before I did anything, I first discussed the matter with the Lord. I rejoiced while I walked, and praised the Lord while I worked. Just as a fish that is used to playing in a small pond experiences the vastness of the sea for the first time, I too came to enjoy the limitless bliss of God.

1949년 가을 우리는 막내 시동생 김문근을 결혼시켰다. 어머님, 아버님이 안 계시는 혼인이라 더욱 정성을 들였다. 그때 우리에게는 100만 원이 있었다. 패물로 금비녀를 준비하는 등 모두 합해서 95만 원이 들었다. 우리의 전 재산을 다 쓰게 되었지만 기쁘기만 했다. 혼인 잔치도 아름답게 차리고 정성을 다 했다. 나는 너무 피로하고 발이 부어서 문지방도 넘지 못할 정도였다. 그 해 1949년 10월 20일, 둘째 딸 정주를 낳았다. 참 귀여웠다.

1950년 6월 25일은 주일이었다. 남산교회에서 이상근 목사님과 나를 보내서 개척한 우리 대봉교회는 교인이 많아짐으로 인해 교회를 짓기 위해서 헌금을 하고 있었다. 그때 잠시 불이 꺼졌다. 나중에 뉴스에서 6·25동란이라고 했다. 참으로 어처구니가 없었다. 해방의 기쁨도 가시지 않은 이때에 같은 동족끼리 서로 죽이는 비극이 났으니 말이다.

그 후 1950년 9월 15일 맥아더 장군이 인천상륙작전에 성공하여, 9월 28일 수도 서울을 수복함으로써 전세는 역전이 되었다. 우리는 남한이 승리한 소식을 듣고 고향인 대구로 돌아왔다. 우리는 피난 보따리를 풀고 교회로 갔다. 반가운 교우들의 얼굴은 더욱 새로웠다. 그때 이상근 목사님은 피난도 가

9. My Brother-in-law's Wedding and the Korean War

In the fall of 1949, my brother-in-law Moon Keun married. Since both of his parents had passed away, Soo Keun and I did our best to take care of everything for him. At that time, we only had one million won, but I wanted to prepare as much as possible. For the bride's jewelry, I bought a gold hair ornament called a *binyeo*, among other things. The total cost of the wedding was 950,000 won. Though I had spent all our savings on my brother-in-law's wedding, I was very happy. I poured my heart into the wedding preparations. Having overworked, my feet got so swollen that I couldn't even take a single step forward. Shortly after, on October 20, 1949, our fourth child and second daughter Jung Joo was born. She was adorable.

The congregation at Daebong Presbyterian Church—a church that I helped Reverend Sang Keun Lee establish and that was commissioned by Namsan Presbyterian Church— was getting bigger, so on June 25, 1950, there was a special offering time for the construction of a larger building. Suddenly, there was a blackout. We heard on the news that the Korean War had started. We were all stunned. With the joy of liberation still fresh in our minds, it was unthinkable that such a tragedy, let alone a brutal battle between brothers, would strike so soon in our nation.

시지 않았다. 끝까지 주님의 양 무리를 지키고 계셨다. 우리 대봉교회는 이북에서 온 피난민으로 꼭 찼다. 또한 전쟁의 상처로 각 병원, 학교는 상이군인으로 가득했다. 우리는 음식을 준비하고 위문품도 가지고 그들을 위문하며 위로했다. 그분들을 위한 전도사도 파송했다. 다리 끊어진 사람, 팔이 잘린 사람, 팔다리가 다 없는 사람 등 당시의 처참함은 이 지면에 다 쓸 수도 없다. 이들은 그나마 다행한 일이었다. 총도 한번 못 만져 본 청년들이 그저 나이가 젊다는 이유 하나만으로 모조리 붙들려 가서 한 부대에 생존자가 극소수일 정도로 처참한 전쟁이었다.

On September 15, 1950, General Douglas MacArthur landed in Incheon. Seoul was regained on September 28, and soon the war was over. We returned home to Daegu. After we unpacked, we went to the church. The happy faces of the members of the congregation were precious. Our minister, Reverend Sang Keun Lee, had not left the city to find refuge but had instead taken care of his flock till the end. Daebong Presbyterian Church was filled with many refugees from North Korea; hospitals and schools were filled with disabled veterans. We visited disabled veterans, bringing them food and other gifts in order to comfort them. We also sent an evangelist to the hospital. Some veterans had lost their legs, others their arms, and some had lost all their limbs. It was truly a miserable sight. Still, they were the fortunate ones. So many young men who had never even picked up a rifle before were drafted, only because they were young. Only a few young men in each unit survived. The war was one big nightmare.

Chapter 2

Every Athlete Exercises
Self – control in All Things

이기기를 다투는 자마다
모든 일에 절제하나니

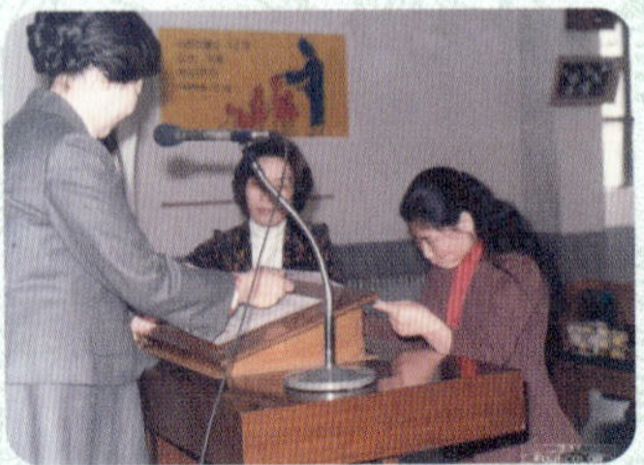

기술 자립 돕는 애우관
House of Friends, shelter for girls (1960s)

대한기독교여자절제회 연합회 회관 완공
The KWCTU Hall, completed (1970)

이화여대 총장을 역임하시고
절제회 고문으로 수고해 주신
김활란 박사님과
With Dr.Helen Kim,
then president of
Ewha Woman's University and
KWCTU council member (1969)

세계기독교여자절제대회들 (Triennial World Conventions of the World Woman's Christian Temperance Union)

28차 영국 세필드 (1980)
The 28th Convention (Sheffield, England)

100주년 미국 시카고 (1983)
The 100th anniversary (Chicago, U.S.A.)

30차 대회 필리핀 마닐라 (1986)
The 30th Convention
(Manila, Philippines)

31차 대회 카나다 에드몬톤. 핀란드 알토 회장 (1989)
With Anja Aalto of Finland at the 31st Convention (Edmonton, Canada)

1. 절제회 가입

"이기기를 다투는 자마다 모든 일에 절제하나니
그들은 썩을 승리자의 관을 얻고자 하되
우리는 썩지 아니할 것을 얻고자 하노라."
(고린도전서 9:25)

하나님을 모신 우리 가정은 어린 한 생명 한 생명이 성령의 충만함을 받고 태어나 착하고 건강하게 자라고 있었다. 남편의 사업도 주님의 축복을 받아 크게 발전했다. 1952년 2월 29일 셋째 아들 영훈이가 태어났다.

하루는 남편이 출장을 가고 없는데 도둑이 들어왔다. 집에 있던 옷을 몽땅 다 가져 갔다. 다음날 아침, 도둑 맞은 것을 발견하고 나는 아이들과 가정 예배를 드리면서 이렇게 말했다. "나는 일찍 모태에서 나서 머리털 하나도 하나님의 허락 없이는 안 빠지는 줄 아는데, 오늘 다 가져 가게 허락하심은 하나님께서 내 겨레를 위해서 일하라는 경고이시다. 너희들은 엄마가 예수님을 믿고 아빠는 부지런히 일하시니 지상낙원에 살고 있다. 그러나 어젯밤에 우리 집에 들어와서 물건을 가져간 불쌍한 이웃들을 위해서 누가 일할꼬?" 하니, 아이들은 다 눈을 빤짝이면서 "우리가 일하지요." 하였다. 나는 "그렇다면 오

1. Joining the KWCTU

25 *"Everyone who competes in the games goes into strict*
training. They do it to get a crown that will not last;
but we do it to get a crown that will last forever."
(1 Corinthians 9:25)

Our family invited God to be the center of our household, and He allowed all my children to be filled with the Holy Spirit from birth and to grow as kindhearted individuals. The Lord also blessed our business. On February 29, 1952, our fifth child and third son, Younghoon, was born.

One night while my husband was away on a business trip, a thief broke into our house and took all of our clothes. The next morning when we realized that our house had been broken into, I gathered my children for family worship.

"Ever since I was born, I knew that not a single strand of my hair would fall out without God's permission," I said to my children, "consider what happened during the night a warning from God to us to start working for His people. You my children live in an earthly paradise because your mom believes in Jesus and your dad works diligently. But who will work for our poor neighbors, like the person who broke into our house and took away all our things?"

"We will work for them," the children said with their

늘 우리는 잃은 것보다 얻은 것이 더 많다.” 하고 감사하며 기도했다. “하나님 아버지! 이 불쌍한 민족을 구원하는 데 저희 가정을 써 주시옵소서. 이 한 생명으로 내 민족이 죄를 회개한다면 찬미하며 바치겠나이다. 예수님 이름으로 기도합니다. 아-멘.”

그때 옆집에는 박귀순 집사님이 살고 계셨다. 그분은 나를 너무도 사랑했으며 나보다 세 살이 위였지만, 믿으신 지 7년밖에 안되어서 늘 나에게 신앙에 대하여 물어왔다. 그날 아침, 우리 집에 간밤에 도둑이 들었다는 소식을 듣고 내가 울고 있을 줄 알고 위로하러 왔다. 예상과 달리 우리 가정이 마가의 다락방과 같이 큰 성령의 불이 붙고 있음을 보았다. 예배를 마치고 나니 이분은 기뻐 춤을 추며, “나는 오늘 아침과 같이 기쁜 날은 처음입니다.” 라고 말했다.

나는 “박 집사님, 지금은 춤출 때가 아니에요. 당신도 사장 부인이요 나도 사장 부인인데, 우리가 대문을 꼭 잠그고 들어앉아 있으면 불쌍한 이 민족을 누가 도울 수 있겠어요? 우리 주머니 끈을 풀고 함께 주님을 위해 헌신하여 불쌍한 이웃을 도웁시다.”하고 말했다. 그 후 나는 박 집사님과 절제회에 가입하여, 바울과 바나바처럼 동역자가 되어 열심히 일했다. 1954년 2월 7일 넷째 아들 영철이가 태어났다.

twinkling eyes.

"Then today, we have gained more than we have lost," I replied. "Heavenly Father, may You use our family in Your ministry to save the poor. May we witness to this nation so that it may come to you with a repentant heart. And for this purpose I offer you my life with praise. In Jesus' name we pray. Amen."

Deaconess Kwi Soon Park, our next door neighbor, loved me very dearly. Though she was three years older than me, she had been a Christian for only seven years. She always asked me questions about faith. Having heard that morning that a thief had broken into our house, she came running through our gates to comfort me, thinking I'd be in tears. Instead she saw that our family was filled with the Holy Spirit, just as were the apostles in Mark's Upper Room. "I've never been this happy before in my life," Deaconess Kwi Soon Park said as she danced.

"This is no time to dance. We, as wives of company presidents, are in a position to help others. If we close our doors and shut people out of our homes, who then will help the poor? Let us loosen our purse strings and help our people," I said. Shortly after, I joined the Korea Woman's Christian Temperance Union (KWCTU) with Mrs. Kwi Soon Park, and like Paul and Barnabas, we worked earnestly together. On February 7, 1954, my sixth child and fourth son, Young Chul, was born.

In 1954, I was appointed as trustee of the Daegu KWCTU.

나는 1954년 대한기독교여자절제회 대구지회 이사로 선정되었다. 전도가 하고 싶어서 반월당이라는 상회에 절제회의 소비조합을 만들고 매일 전도지를 뿌렸다. 자라게 하시는 분은 우리 하나님이시니, 우리는 부지런히 뿌렸다. 나는 전쟁으로 파괴된 이 가난한 나라에 절제운동이 제일 절실하게 필요한 운동임을 뼈저리게 느꼈다. 우리는 대구에 절제회관이 건립되도록 열심히 일했다. 1956년 막내딸 성주가 태어났다. 우리 집은 귀한 자녀들을 하나님께로부터 선물 받아 무척이나 행복했다.

아직 6·25동란의 상처가 가시지 않았다. 고아들이 많아서 고아원들이 다 수용할 수 없었다. 12세가 되면 고아원을 떠나 자립을 해야 했다. 이렇게 나온 아이들은 거처가 없으니 다리 밑에서 자면서, 낮에는 구두를 닦고 밤이면 범죄를 저지르곤 했다.

대구 절제회는 이런 아이들을 구하기로 의논했다. 우리는 1962년 하나님의 축복으로 많은 눈물의 수고 끝에 삼덕교회 건너편에 팔백만 원을 주고 절제회관을 구입했다. 먼저 하나님께 감사 예배를 드리고, 고아원에서 나온 아이들을 모아 놓고 야간에 중학교 과정을 공부시켰다. 그리고 모자를 쓰게 해서 이들을 사랑해 주니 그들은 너무도 기뻐했다. 선생님은 각

I was very eager to witness about Christ. The members and I opened a consumers' co-op at one corner of a shop called Banwoldang and distributed tracts every day, knowing that if we sowed the seeds, the Lord would let them grow. I was convinced that the temperance movement was needed in this country, which was still impoverished by the war. We worked diligently to build the KWCTU Hall. On November 19, 1956, my seventh child and youngest daughter, Sung Joo, was born. My husband and I were extremely happy that God had blessed us with the gift of seven children.

The wounds inflicted by the Korean War still hadn't been healed. Too many children had lost their parents, and orphanages couldn't accommodate them all. Children were permitted to stay only until the age of twelve where then they were expected to live on their own. Having no real place to call home, these children slept under bridges and made a living shining shoes during the day, and some engaged in crime by night.

The Daegu KWCTU reached out to these children. By God's abundant blessing, and after much tearful effort, we bought a building across from Samduk Presbyterian Church for eight million won in 1962, to use as the KWCTU Hall. The first thing we did was worship the Lord with a thanksgiving service. Then we gathered some of the children who had left their orphanages, and we started a night school

교회에서 은혜 받은 대학생들로 구성이 되었다. 이 아이들은 구두를 닦으면서 욕밖에는 들은 것이 없는 아이들이었다. 이 사님들이 자녀와 같이 사랑을 쏟으니 이 아이들은 냉정한 사회에도 한줄기 희망이 있음을 깨닫게 되었다.

"우리 죄를 회개하고 예수님의 보혈로 죄 사함 받고, 성령 충만함을 받으라."고, 부흥 목사님들이 오셔서 외치면, 아이들은 통회하고 자복했다. 아이들의 삶에 매일 변화가 일어났다. 남의 돈을 훔치려던 마음에 그리스도께서 임하시니, 매일 진실하게 일하고 밤이면 공부하고 주님의 말씀을 배웠다. 2년 속성반으로 중학 과정을 마치고 취직도 했다. 길 잃은 양들이 주님 품으로 돌아와 참 길을 찾게 된 것이다.

for middle school kids. The children were overwhelmed by the love we showed them. The teachers were from different churches and were university students who had experienced the grace of the Lord. Shining shoes for a living, the children had only been exposed to abusive words and were poorly addressed by the greater public. But because the KWCTU trustees loved them as their own children, the children came to realize that a ray of hope still existed in this cruel world.

We also invited evangelists who preached, "Repent, receive forgiveness through the precious blood of Jesus, and be filled with the Holy Spirit." These young children repented, confessing their sins. There was a great transformation in their lives. Even their goals in life had now changed. Many had only been interested in stealing money from others, but now, having become Christians, they worked hard during the day and studied at night to learn the Word of God. After two years of intensive study, they finished middle school and found better jobs. Many young lost souls returned to the Lord and found the true way of life.

2. 서울의 절제회관

　　남편의 사업이 확장되어 서울로 이사를 오게 되었다. 서울에 와서 보니 여기는 연합회 본부인데도 절제회관이 없었다. 연세대학교 창설자 언더우드 박사님의 아들 원한경 박사님의 부인, 에텔 언더우드이사가 벽돌 이층집을 사서, 절제회 이사로 계시면서 이 집을 절제회관 겸 형무소에서 나온 아이들을 수용하여 선도하는 데 사용하게 하셨다. 그 후 그 분이 돌아가시고 새문안교회에서 교육관을 짓는다고 하니, 언더우드 박사님 자제인 원일한 박사님이 그 집을 새문안교회에 어머님 이름으로 기증하셨다. 이제 야단이 났다. 절제회에서는 우리가 사회사업을 위해서 10년을 썼으니 법으로 해서도 우리 것이라고 하고, 새문안교회에서는 집문서를 정식으로 연보로 받았으니 자기 집이라고 했다.

　　나는 서울로 이사 온 직후, 이 소식을 듣고 철야기도를 드렸다. 이 일을 지나치면 주님의 이름에 큰 해가 되겠고, 이 일을 떠맡으려고 하니 서울에 처음 와 낯선 내가 큰 고생을 할 것이 분명했다. 그러나 내가 고생함으로 주님께 영광이 된다면 아무리 힘들더라고 이 일을 해야 한다는 깨달음이 왔다. 그래서 새벽녘에 "하나님 아버지! 주님의 십자가를 달게 지겠습니다."라고 기도드렸다.

2. The KWCTU Hall in Seoul

Our family moved to Seoul because Soo Keun was looking to expand his business. There was no KWCTU Hall in Seoul, though the headquarters was located there. Ethel Van Wagoner Underwood—one of the KWCTU trustees and whose husband was Dr. Horace Horton Underwood, son of the founder of Yonsei University—bought a two-story brick house to use as the KWCTU office and to accommodate poor girls who were released from prison. After she passed away, her son—Dr. Horace Grant Underwood—donated the house to Saemoonan Presbyterian Church in memory of his mother. This led to a dispute because the KWCTU claimed that the house belonged to them since their social work had been conducted there for the past ten years. Saemoonan Presbyterian Church, on the other hand, asserted that the house belonged to them since the deed to the house was in their possession.

I prayed all night after hearing the news, for if this conflict were to remain unresolved, the name of our Lord would be disgraced. Yet I knew that I would have a hard time living in this new city were I to take the lead in settling the issue. Regardless, I made up my mind to undertake the task of resolving the dispute, as I realized that my hardship might be used to bring glory, however trivial the situation might be, to God. "God our Father, I will gladly bear Your cross," I prayed.

그 다음날 나는 절제회에 가서 다음과 같이 설교했다.

"여러분! 우리가 한국 사람의 집을 10년이나 썼으면 집세가 얼마나 많았겠습니까? 그 동안 잘 썼으니 감사하다고 생각하세요. 그리고 이 집이 바쳐지는 곳이 교회이니 기쁨으로 드립시다. 그리고 우리들의 주머니 끈을 풉시다. 어느 때까지 우리 한국 사람은 남의 도움만 받겠습니까? 이제 초가집이면 초가집, 기와집이면 기와집, 빌딩이면 빌딩, 하나님께서 주시는 대로 받읍시다."

내가 이렇게 설교를 마치자, 절제회의 모든 회원들이 큰 감명을 받고 뜻을 같이해 주었다. 이제 집 때문에 교회와 재판할 걱정은 끝났다. 우리는 그 자리에서 헌금을 했다. 비록 큰 돈은 아니었지만 하나님의 은혜가 가득했다.

그 후 나는 김활란 박사님을 만나 뵈러 갔다. 내가 절제회를 하게 된 동기와 이 민족에게 꼭 필요한 운동임을 말씀드렸더니, 한 30분간 말씀드리는 중에 그는 성령의 감동을 받아 자기 생명이 있는 한 무엇이나 협력하겠다고 하셨다. 이제 한국의 제일 귀한 여성 지도자이시며 세계적으로도 명성이 높으신 귀한 동역자를 하나님께서 우리에게 허락해 주셨다. 나는 주 안에서 너무도 기뻤다. 김활란 박사님을 절제회의 고문으로 모시고 자주 의논을 드렸다. 박사님은 늘 최선을 다해서 협

The next day, I went to the KWCTU meeting and addressed the members:

All the members of the KWCTU listened attentively to the sermon. All was settled. There was no worry about lawsuits over possession of the building. We made an offering and, though our offerings weren't much, God's grace filled the room. The spirit of strife left us.

Afterwards, I went to meet Dr. Helen Kim, the first Korean president of Ewha Woman's University. I described to her in thirty minutes my involvement in the KWCTU and the necessity of the temperance movement for this country. As I talked to her, she was moved by the Holy Spirit. She told me that she would help in every possible way for as long as she

조해주셨고, 자주 우리 집에 모시게 되었다. 김활란 박사님은 친구분들께 여귀옥 이사는 이름 그대로 귀한 보화와 같은 사람이라고 소개하시며 부족한 나를 참으로 소중히 여기고 사랑해 주셨다.

lived. God gave me one of the most precious woman leaders in Korea as a coworker. It was a time for rejoicing in the Lord. She was a KWCTU advisor, so we often discussed various matters. She always did her utmost to help. When speaking to her friends about me, she would say, "Mrs. Kwi Ok Yeu is as precious as a jewel, just like her name." Though I was unworthy, Dr. Helen Kim really loved and cared about me.

3. 절제회 열두 제자 모임과 절제회관 구입

그 후 나는 절제회관 구입 기금을 장만하기 위해서 '열두 제자 모임'이라는 그룹을 만들었다. 50만 원씩 하는 계 형식의 모임으로, 성경공부와 함께 했다. 제일 먼저 매영숙 장로님 아드님의 컨트리클럽에서 모였다. 그때 김활란 박사님이 우리에게 설교해 주셨다. 김활란 박사님은 퍽 연로하셨는데, 주님의 사업에는 먼 길도 사양하지 않고 오셔서 베풀어 주신 사랑을 생각하면 지금도 아름다운 추억이 된다.

당시 열두 제자 모임 멤버로 있던 최 사장 부인에게서, 자기 집이 한 채 더 있다고 하며 그 집을 사서 절제회관으로 사용하면 어떻겠냐는 전화가 왔다. 나는 "지금 우리 절제회는 돈도 없고 아직 집을 살 단계가 못됩니다." 라고 말했다. 그분은 전화를 또 해주면서 돈은 천천히 내도 된다고 했다. 이유인즉, 그 집을 팔아서 집을 하나 지으려고 하니 돈은 일시에 지불하지 않아도 된다고 하였다. 이 일도 하나님의 뜻이라고 생각하고 그 부인과 함께 집을 둘러보았다. 집은 저택인데 회관으로 쓰기에는 너무 누추해서 "부인, 나는 이렇게 좋은 집에 사는데 하나님을 위한 집이 너무 누추해서 안 되겠습니까." 하고 사양했다. 그 부인은 수리만 하면 회관으로 쓰기에 좋을 것이라고 계속 권유했다. 하도 열심히 말하니 서울에 처음 온 나는 매영

3. The Twelve Disciples' Club and the Purchase of the KWCTU Hall

I formed a small Bible study group called the Twelve Disciples' Club for KWCTU members. Through this club we raised funds to buy a hall for the KWCTU in Seoul. It was somewhat like a *gye*—a traditional Korean support system of mutual financing for women whereby each woman, usually out of ten members, deposits a fixed sum of money each month, and they take turns using the whole monthly deposit, perhaps for a child's wedding expenses. Our first meeting was held at a country club that belonged to the son of Mrs. Young Sook Mae, an elderwoman. Dr. Helen Kim gave a touching sermon; the times I spent with her will always remain as beautiful memories.

The next day, I received a telephone call from Mrs. Choi, a member of the Twelve Disciples' Club. She said that she had an extra house she wanted us to buy for the KWCTU. I told her, "The KWCTU is still short on funds; we can't afford your house." She called me again and said we didn't need to pay her right away, that we could make installment payments. Believing it might be God's will, I went to see the house. "It is big enough, but I'm afraid it's not up to my standards. I live in a nice house and this one seems too broken down for us to dedicate as the house of the Lord," I said and refused to buy it. Mrs. Choi insisted that with a little repair, the house would make a nice office building,

숙 이사님을 모시고 다시 그 집을 찾아갔다. 집 주변 환경을 몰랐던 내가 "매 장로님! 여기가 어디입니까?"하고 여쭈니, 매 장로님 대답이 "여기가 서울역전입니다."하셨다. 나는 그 말에 너무도 반갑고 감사했다. "하나님 아버지! 감사합니다. 이 처소가 말세에 노아의 방주가 되게 해 주시옵소서. 이 서울 장안이 무서운 곳인 줄도 모르고 시골 처녀들이 무작정 보따리를 들고 매일 수도 없이 서울로 올라와서 죄악으로 빠지고 있는데, 이 집이 이들을 구원하는 방주가 되게 해 주시옵소서." 하고 기도드렸다.

나는 곧 그 집을 사겠다고 그 부인에게 전했다. 그때 우리는 50만 원밖에 없었는데, 그 집 대금이 550만 원이었다. 나는 그 날부터 준비를 시작했다. 언더우드 박사님을 찾아가서 우리가 폐를 안 끼치려고 열두 제자 모임도 가지고 있는데 죽어가는 생명을 구하기 위해서 일찍 집을 사려고 하니, 원 박사님도 좀 힘을 합하는 것이 우리 회원들에게 좋은 인상도 주고 선한 일에 도움이 되겠다고 설명하자, 기쁜 마음으로 50만 원을 협조해 주셨다. 며칠이 안되어 우리는 190만 원을 모았다. 나머지 10만 원을 위해서 김환란 박사님께 말씀 드렸더니 기쁜 마음으로 헌금해 주셨다. 바로 다음날, 열두 제자 모임의 날이었다. 이 모임 후에 회관을 계약하기로 했다. 나는 성경

especially since it was at a good location. Since I didn't know the geographical location very well, not having lived in Seoul for very long, I went there once more with Mrs. Young Sook Mae. I asked, "Where exactly is the location of the house?" and was told, "Right in front of Seoul Station." The location was perfect! I prayed: "Heavenly Father! Thank you! May this house be like Noah's ark. Many girls from the countryside come to Seoul every day, not knowing how dangerous it is to live in the city. These young girls often fall into a pit of sin. May this house be an ark that saves the souls of many people."

I told Mrs. Choi that we would buy the house. It cost 5.5 million won, but we only had 500,000 won. I immediately began my efforts to collect money. I visited Dr. Horace Grant Underwood and explained to him that we had formed the Twelve Disciples' Club in order not to burden others any longer. I told him that we planned to buy the house as soon as possible, for we wanted to save lost, dying souls. I also told him that his cooperation would encourage our members in doing the Lord's work. Glad to help us, he gave us 500,000 won. In just a few days, we collected 1.9 million won. We were only short 100,000 won of the down payment. When I asked Dr. Helen Kim if she would donate 100,000 won, with a glad heart, she willingly did so. The Twelve Disciples' Club was scheduled to meet the next day, at which the contract for the house would be written. I was to deliver

말씀도 전하게 되어 있었다. 거기는 믿지 않는 부인이 다섯 명이나 있었다. 일석이조의 역할이 시작된 귀중한 시간이었다. 곧 절제회관 구입을 위해 모금도 하고, 믿지 않는 상류층 부인들에게 전도도 할 수 있는 기회가 된 것이다.

이 모임 며칠 전, 나는 우리 회의의 기둥 역할을 해주시는 이사님을 찾아갔다. "이사님, 우리가 열두 제자 모임이라고 모였지만 모두 돈을 다 찾아 가면 우리는 헛수고만 하는 것입니다. 이사님과 나는 이 50만 원이 없어도 살 수 있으니, 오병이어와 같이 50만 원씩 회관을 위해 내어놓읍시다." 하고 권했다. 그분이 기쁘게 승낙해서 나는 참 기뻤다. 이 한 사람이라도 협조하면 나는 좀 힘이 되겠다고 생각했다. 그런데 그 후 다시 같은 자리에서 그분은 내게 자기는 그 돈을 낼 수 없다는 것이었다. 나는 하도 기가 막혀서 "딴 회원들이 벌써 다 듣고 감사하다고 했는데, 안 내시면 이사님 인격에 해가 됩니다. 돈 50만 원은 있어도 살고 없어도 살지만 인격이 더 귀하지 않습니까?" 하고 말했다. 그러나 그분은 아무런 반응이 없었다.

며칠 후 열두 제자 모임과 동시에 집을 계약할 약속의 날이 닥쳐왔다. 내가 모든 부인들을 나의 집에 오게 하여 식사를 시작하려고 하는데 이사님이 들어왔다. 그는 화가 난 목소리로 "나는 이 모임을 안 하겠으니 돈을 내놓으시오." 하고 말했다.

a message from the Word of God. And since five non-Christian members had joined the Club, that particular meeting served two purposes: to raise funds for the purchase of the house and to witness Christ to the five non-Christian upper-class members.

Several days before the meeting, I went to see one of the members, whom I'll call Mrs. M. "Mrs. M, the Twelve Disciple's Club was founded with the purpose to raise funds to buy a hall for the KWCTU. But if our members all decide to use their *gye* earnings for their own purpose, all our efforts will be in vain. You and I can live without the 500,000 won *gye* earnings we would receive. Let us offer 500,000 won each and witness the miracle of the five loaves of bread and two fish." I was very glad when she said yes. I felt that as long as one member cooperated, I could find great strength. But when I met her days later, she said she no longer wished to offer up her *gye* money. "You're putting your reputation on the line," I said in shock. "All the members have already thanked you for your generosity and they are counting on you to follow through. I am sure you can live without the 500,000 won, but isn't your reputation much more valuable?" Mrs. M didn't say a word.

The day had come for the Twelve Disciple's Club to gather for our monthly meeting and to finalize our contract for the house. I invited the members to my home for lunch. Just as we were about to start our meal, Mrs. M burst into

나는 "왜 그러십니까?" 하고 물었더니, 그분 대답이 "여자들이 50만 원이라는 큰 계를 계속할 수도 없고 돈도 없는데, 오늘 계약을 한다니 다 불가능한 일이라서 나는 이 모임에서 탈퇴해야겠소." 하고 말했다. 그의 얼굴에는 분노가 가득 차있었다. 우리 이 사진들만 있어도 야단인데, 하물며 지금 믿지 않는 부인이 다섯 명이나 와서 주님의 복음을 듣기 위해 앉아 있지 않는가!

나는 속으로 하나님께 기도드렸다. "하나님 아버지, 이 일을 어떻게 하면 좋을까요? 제가 만약 이분에게 한마디라도 한다면, 오늘 회관 계약도 안 되고 안 믿는 부인들은 믿는 사람도 별수 없다 하고 다 가버리면 그만입니다. 이 열두 제자 모임을 모으는데도 몇 달이 걸렸는데, 모든 것이 허사요, 주님의 영광을 가리우게 되었습니다. 저를 도와주세요. 예수님 이름으로 기도합니다. 아-멘." 나는 그때 마귀의 권세를 대적하는 데는 성경 말씀밖에 없다는 것을 기억하고 이렇게 대답했다. "이사님! 내가 만약 이사님께 실수가 있었다 하더라도, 예수님을 믿는 우리는 자기에게 잘못한 자를 용서하는 것이 도리입니다." 그 이사님은 교회의 장로이며 교회도 많이 세우고 일을 많이 하신 분이라, 이 말을 듣고 자기가 성경대로 행동하지 않았음을 그 자리에서 수긍하셨다.

그제야 우리는 식사를 시작했다. 그분은 한 그릇을 다 잡수

the room. She was so angry that she looked as though she were possessed by an evil spirit. "I will no longer be a part of the Club, so give me all my money back," she said angrily. "Women cannot afford to take part in a 500,000 won *gye* every month, and it's impossible to sign a contract when you don't have money!"

I prayed quietly inside: "Heavenly Father, what am I to do? If I argue with her, the contract will be doomed, and the five women who are not Christian will leave with the impression that Christians aren't so different from nonbelievers. It took so many months just to start the Twelve Disciples' Club. Please do not allow anything to go wrong or overshadow Your glory. Please help me, Lord. In Jesus' name I pray. Amen." I then remembered that in order to fight against Satan, there was nothing more powerful than the Word of God. "Dear friend, if I have sinned against you in any way, please forgive me, for while unbelievers attack those who wrong them, we believers have to forgive them." Since Mrs. M was an elderwoman at church and had helped in building new churches and doing a lot of good work, she soon realized that she hadn't acted according to the Word of God.

We then started our meal. I couldn't swallow anything as tears fell like rain. I delivered my sermon. The evil spirit's stronghold departed from the room and the Holy Spirit began anointing the whole session with His abundant grace. The

셨다. 그러나 나는 눈물이 비 오듯 흘러서 밥이 입에 들어가지 않았다. 나는 설교를 시작했다. 그때 성령의 역사가 임하여서 큰 은혜의 시간이 되었다. 예배가 끝나고 모든 사람은 돌아가고 김성무 회장님과 나, 그리고 집을 팔 부인과 성내던 이사님만 옆방으로 갔다. 이사님은 다시 성이 났다. 그때서야 나는 말했다. "이사님, 이제 당신의 돈 50만 원은 필요 없습니다. 하나님께서 무에서 세계도 지으셨는데, 550만 원짜리 집, 당신의 성난 돈을 안 받으셔도 조금도 부족함이 없습니다." 그때 김성무 회장님이 내 얼굴에 평강의 빛이 빛나고 있었다고 했다. 그 후부터 김성무 회장님은 나를 생명같이 사랑하셨다.

계약을 마치고 돌아오는 차 안에서 집을 매매한 부인이 내게 말했다. "나는 오늘 내 집을 팔아도 만약 그이가 내게 그렇게 무례한 행동을 했다면 안 팝니다. 그런데 어째서 당신의 집도 아니고 공공 회관을 사시면서 그런 모욕을 당하고 참습니까?" 하고 심각하게 물었다. 나는 "예수님을 믿으면 참을 수 있습니다. 지금 그분이 성을 낸 것은 그분이 낸 것이 아니고, 오늘 하나님께 영광이 되고 불쌍한 여성들을 위해서 노아의 방주와 같은 집터를 사려고 하니까 악한 영이 뒤에서 훼방을 놓은 것입니다." 하고 대답했다. 그분은 그 말을 듣고 "부인, 나도 예수님을 믿겠습니다. 나뿐만 아니라 우리 온 가정이 다

meeting ended and everyone went home, except for the KWCTU president, Mrs. Sung Moo Kim; Mrs. Choi, who was selling the house; Mrs. M; and me. We went into the next room. Mrs. M got angry again. Gently but surely, I spoke to her again. "Mrs. M," I began, "we don't need your angry 500,000 won. God created the world from scratch. He can buy this 5.5 million won house without your money." Mrs. Sung Moo Kim told me afterwards that my face shined with peace when I said those words. She loved me dearly.

On our way back from the notary's office, Mrs. Choi said: "Dear friend, I sold my house today, but if Mrs. M had acted so impolitely towards me, I wouldn't have sold it. How is it that you remained patient in spite of her fit of anger? Besides, you're not even buying the house for yourself but as a building for public use." I answered: "If you believe in Jesus, you can be patient in situations such as this. The anger didn't come from her but from the devil, who tried to destroy our plan to buy the office for the KWCTU, for the devil knew we were going to use the house like Noah's ark, to save poor girls and to bring glory to God." Mrs. Choi replied: "I want to believe in Jesus! Not only I but my family will believe in Jesus." She had heard the calling of the Holy Spirit. *Hallelujah!* I thought. The devil was trying to create problems so that we would not be able to buy the house for the KWCTU, but God not only let us buy it but also saved Mrs. Choi's family. That day, I earned much more than I had

믿겠습니다.” 라고 말했다. “할렐루야!” 마귀는 회관을 못 사게 방해했지만, 하나님께서는 이 회관뿐만 아니라 최 사장님 한 가정을 구원하는 역사까지 허락하셨다. 오늘 나는 잃은 것보다 얻은 것이 더 많은 날이었다. 그 후 열두 제자 모임이 끝날 때는 안 믿던 부인 네 명도 다 믿게 되었다.

우리는 200만 원에 계약은 걸었지만 중도금 250만 원을 2월 말까지 지급하게 되어있었다. 아무리 애를 써도 100만 원밖에 되지 않아 150만 원을 장만하기가 어려웠다. 지금 같으면 얼마 안 되지만 그때는 매우 큰 돈이었다.

생각하다 못해 우리 이사님 중 한 분인 선교사 모진주 씨를 방문했다. 우리가 방문한 목적을 이야기하며, 선교부에 돈이 있으면 150만 원만 무이자로 빌렸으면 좋겠다고 말했다. 그분은 눈이 둥그래졌다. “그런 큰돈을 우리는 만져 볼 수도 없지요.” 하셨다. 나는 어찌나 미안했던지 인사를 하고 나오려다가, “모 부인, 당신이 본국에 편지를 한장 쓸 수 있지요? 한국의 부인들이 선한 주의 사업을 하다가 기금이 모자라서 애쓰고 있다는 말을 전해주십시오.”라고 말했다. 모 부인은 “그것은 할 수 있습니다.” 라고 대답했다. 나는 “네, 그럼 부탁합니다.”하고 인사하고 총총히 돌아왔다. 2월은 닥쳐오는데 아무런 소식이 없었다. 나는 모 부인이 불가능한 것처럼 말해서 모

lost. By the time the Twelve Disciples' Club folded, four of the unbelieving women became Christians.

The KWCTU was able to pay the 2 million won down payment, but we still had to collect 2.5 million won by February. We were hopeful about collecting an additional 1 million won, but collecting the entire 2.5 million won was beyond our capacity. This was a great deal of money back then.

After much consideration, we visited Mrs. Margaret Moore, the wife of the missionary Reverend Moore. We told her about the purpose of our visit. We asked her if we could borrow 1.5 million won without interest from the missionary association. "The association has never seen that much money, nor could it afford to give out such a large amount of money," she said with her eyes wide open. I felt terribly sorry and was going to leave, but a thought occurred to me. "Perhaps you can write a letter to your country and explain that some Christian Korean sisters are having a hard time doing God's work due to a lack of funds," I suggested. "That I can do for you," Mrs. Moore replied. February came, but no news had come. I had completely forgotten about my visit to Mrs. Moore's home because she had made it clear that finding us funding would probably be impossible.

That year, my second- and third-born wrote their entrance exams for Seoul National University. Nevertheless, my heart wasn't heavy because of that but because we only had a few days to pay the rest of the money for the house. Late one

부인을 방문했던 것은 잊어버리고 있었다.

그 해에 서울대학교에 나의 둘째 아들과 큰딸이 입학 시험을 쳤다. 나의 마음은 절제회관 대금 지급으로 무겁기만 했다. 며칠 있으면 중도금도 치러야 하는데 밤 늦게 전화가 왔다. 김성무 회장님의 전화였다. "여 이사님, 나는 괴롭습니다. 당신은 이사인데도 이렇게 힘을 쓰는데 나는 회장으로서 조금도 도울 수 없으니 안타깝습니다." 하신다. 나는 동정이 되었다. "회장님, 주무세요. 인간의 할 도리를 다하면 하나님의 기적이 나타납니다. 우리는 최선을 다했습니다. 오늘, 내일, 모레, 삼일 동안에 이적이 나타날 것입니다." 하고 대답했다. 1만원도 못 내시는 형편에 150만 원을 걱정하고 계신 김성무 회장님의 안타까운 말을 듣고 한 말이었다. 김성무 회장님은 그 전화를 받고 편히 잠을 주무셨다고 한다.

나는 요셉과 같이 의미심장한 꿈을 잘 꾼다. 그 후 어느 날 밤 꿈을 꾸는데, 내가 어린 아이를 업고 길을 걷고 있었다. 저 먼 바다에서 구름이 하얗게 떠 있었다. '구름이 하늘에 있지 않고 왜 바다에 있지?' 하며 가까이 갔더니 그것은 구름이 아니고 벚꽃이었다 온 바다에 아름다운 벚꽃이 만발하였다, 나는 너무도 기뻐서 한 잎을 따서 머리에 꽂고 또 한 잎을 따서 손에 들었다. 며칠 있으면 우리 집에 김활란 박사님과 절제회

night, I got a phone call from Mrs. Sung Moo Kim. "I feel so bad. You are working so hard as a trustee, but I, the president of the Union, can't help you much." "Sleep well, Mrs. Kim," I replied. "If we do everything we possibly can as human beings, God will start working miracles. Since we are doing our best, there'll be a miracle in three days." There she was, worrying about how to gather 1.5 million won for the KWCTU when she didn't even have 10,000 won to spare. I felt compassion toward her. She said she slept well that night.

Like Joseph in the Bible, I often had dreams. One night in my dream, I was walking along a road, carrying a baby on my back. I came upon the sea and saw a huge white cloud over it. *Why is the cloud on the sea and not in the sky?* I wondered. As I walked closer, I discovered that it was a cherry tree in bloom, not a cloud. The entire sea was covered with cherry blossoms. I was so happy that I picked two flowers. I pinned one in my hair and held the other in my hand. Returning home, I thought of how nice it would be if the cherry trees at our house were in full bloom too, for then Dr. Helen Kim and the other KWCTU trustees would see how beautiful the blossoms are when they were over for the next scheduled meeting. When I opened the gate to our house, the trees were in full bloom all over the yard.

I was really happy when I woke up from the dream. I said to my son Young Min and my daughter Young Joo, who

이사님들이 오시는데 우리 집에도 벚꽃이 피었으면 좋겠다고
소망하고 집으로 돌아왔다. 대문을 여니 우리 온 마당에도 벚
꽃이 만발했다.

나는 잠을 깨고 기쁜 나머지, "애들아, 머리에 꽃을 꽂는
것은 영광의 상징이니 너희 둘 중에 한 사람은 대학에 톱으로
들어가고 한 사람은 거저 합격을 하겠어." 하고 꿈을 해몽하면
서, "바다의 벚꽃은 무엇을 가리킬까?" 하고 궁금해 했다. 며
칠이 못 되어서 큰딸 영주가 서울 미대 수석합격을 했다고 신
문기자들이 달려왔다. 영민이도 서울 문리대에 합격했다. 집
안은 온통 잔치 분위기였다.

바로 그 날은 김활란 박사님과 우리 절제회원들이 모이는
날이었다. 아침에 일찍 일어나서 손님 대접을 위해 분주하게
준비하고 있었다. 그때 절제회에서 전화가 왔다. "여 이사님,
미국에서 5,000불이 왔어요." 했다. 나는 너무도 반가워서
"무슨 돈이?" 하고 물었다. 대답하는 말이, "모 부인이 보낸
편지를 받은 교회에서 왔어요." 한다. 알고 보니 그때 모 부인
의 편지를 받은 교회의 한 중국 부인이 운명하시면서 평생에
모은 5,000불을 목사님께 드리며, 이 돈은 본 교회에 쓰지 말
고 선교지에서 필요하다는 소식이 오면 보내달라고 유언을 했
다는 것이다. 목사님은 바로 그때 모 부인으로부터 편지를 받

were waiting confirmation of their acceptance to Seoul National University: "Dear children, both of you will be accepted to the university. One of you will enter with top results, for in my dream I put a flower—which is the symbol of glory—in my hair." *But what does the sea covered with cherry blossoms symbolize?* we all wondered. After a few days, many journalists flocked to our house because my daughter Young Joo had passed the entrance exam to the College of Fine Arts at Seoul National University with top results. Young Min had also been accepted to Seoul National University. Our house was filled with joy.

That same day, Dr. Helen Kim and all the members from the KWCTU were supposed to gather at our house. I got up early in the morning to get an early start on preparing to receive the guests. I got a phone call from a KWCTU treasurer. "Guess what? Five thousand dollars was sent from the United States," the treasurer said. "From who?" I excitedly asked. "It was sent by the church Mrs. Moore wrote to," she replied. We found out that a Chinese sister who worshipped at the American church had just passed away. She left a life savings of $5,000 towards missions, and her will specified that her home church not use the money but instead wait to receive a request for funds from abroad. Apparently, just when the church was searching mission fields in need of funding, Mrs. Moore's letter arrived at the church. The pastor was sure that God meant for this money

고, 이 돈은 분명히 하나님께서 한국 절제회로 보내라는 뜻임을 깨닫게 되어 보내신 것이었다. 우리는 아직도 그 중국 부인의 이름을 모른다. 하나님께서 베푸신 기적이었다. 꿈에 본 바다의 벚꽃은 바로 이 기쁜 소식의 상징이었다.

우리는 그 5,000불로 중도금을 다 치르고도 25만 원이 남아서 나중에 집수리까지 마쳤다. 하나님의 축복은 이렇게 차고도 넘치는 축복이다. 우리는 몇 달 후 550만 원을 다 지급하고 불쌍한 애우관 아이들을 데리고 그 집으로 이사했다. 애우관은 시골에서 서울로 무작정 상경하는 시골 처녀들이 유혹에 넘어가 사창가에 끌려가지 않도록 미연에 방지하고 저들을 보호하고 교육하는 기관이다. 이렇게 해서 대한기독교여자절제회 연합회 회관이 처음으로 이 땅에 생기게 되었다.

한국에 절제회관을 세우고 난지 얼마 후인 1968년, 일본에서 세계절제대회가 개최되었다. 세계절제회의 여러 나라 대표들이 한국을 방문했을 때 우리는 새로운 회관에서 환영회를 가졌다. 나는 무척 감사했다. 만약 우리가 이 회관을 구하지 않았다면 어찌할 뻔 했던가. 그러나 세계적 기관으로서의 역할을 하기에는 아직 미약한 건물 구조이고 그에 따른 국가 위신에도 문제가 없지 않았다. 그래서 우리는 한번 더 힘을 모아 이 집을 헐고 새 회관을 건축하기로 했다.

to be sent to the KWCTU. To this day, we do not know the name of the Chinese sister, but we are very thankful. It was truly a miracle from God. The cherry blossoms that covered the sea in my dream signified this joyful news.

We were able to pay the remainder of the cost of the house with the $5,000 we received. Even after paying, we still had about 250,000 won remaining, so we repaired the house with that money. God greatly blessed us. We had made the 5.5 million won payment in full within a matter of months. We moved a group of girls into the House of Friends shelter, an outreach program and institution established by the KWCTU, designed to help girls who come to Seoul from the countryside not be lured into prostitution. And the first ever KWCTU Hall was opened in Seoul.

In 1968, soon after we bought the house for the KWCTU, the WWCTU world convention was held in Tokyo, Japan. Many delegates from different countries visited Korea after the convention and we held a reception for them in our new KWCTU Hall. I thanked God. Imagining where we would've invited our visitors if we hadn't bought the house, I thanked God again with a grateful heart. Still, we felt that the structure of the house seemed unsuitable to house the headquarters of such a big international organization, so the KWCTU members decided to unite our efforts once more to reconstruct a new KWCTU Hall.

4. 절제회관 건축 도중에 받은 은혜

회관 구입 후 꼭 3년 만에 다시 건축이 시작되었다. 그러나 김활란 박사님께서 말씀해주신 것처럼 사람의 단체와 같이 약한 곳도 없었다. 모일 회관이 없고 일할 사람이 없으면 해산되고 만다. 빌딩을 지으려고 재정을 점검해 보니 정말 미약했다. 그러나 다시 한번 하나님을 믿고 시작했다. 나에게 아무도 협력할 기미가 보이지 않았다. 부자니까 자기가 다 하겠지 하는 식이었다. 한국 여성은 경제권이 없다. 남편은 아직 믿음이 초보단계였고 유교식 사고의 오랜 관습이 남아, 여성들이 사회에 나가서 일하는 것을 별로 기뻐하지 않았다. 그러므로 나는 남편이 신경 쓰지 않게 하려고 늘 지혜롭게 일해야 했다.

지하실을 파 놓고 인부들은 당장 돈을 달라고 아우성이었다. 내겐 충분한 현금이 없으니 엄청난 시련이었다. 너무 걱정한 나머지 그 다음 주일날 교회에 갔더니 온 몸에 식은땀이 비와 같이 쏟아지고 있었다. 그때 둘째 딸 정주에게 "정주야! 내가 아무래도 이상해. 설교 말씀만 마치면 집으로 가자."고 했다. 설교가 끝나 밖으로 먼저 나오는데, 몇 발자국 못 가서 나는 의식을 잃었다. 2,000명이 넘는 교인들의 찬송 소리가 조금도 들리지 않았다. 정신을 차리고 보니 정주는 울고 서 있었다. 나는 의무실로 옮겨져 한참 동안 안정을 취한 후 집으로

4. The Grace I Received in Constructing the KWCTU Hall

The construction of the new KWCTU hall started three years after we bought the house. Dr. Helen Kim had once told me that the weakest unit is the organization; that if you don't have a hall or any members in it, the organization naturally ceases to exist. She was right. I felt helpless in the beginning as I saw how little money we had available for the construction of the hall. But I initiated the work, for I trusted that God, as He had before, would provide for us again. Nobody showed any interest in helping me. Many assumed that since my husband was rich, I would build the hall by myself. Korean women don't have much economic power. Soo Keun was a newborn Christian and, because of his long-accepted Confucian ethics, he found it difficult to see women in the workforce, let alone away from the domestic domain, so I had to be wise in making decisions so as not to disturb my husband.

As soon as the workers dug the basement area, they demanded their wages. I was confronted with countless difficulties because of lack of money. I was under so much stress and pressure that I began to sweat profusely at church the next Sunday. I was with Jung Joo, my second daughter. "Jung Joo, I don't feel too good. I think I should return home right after the sermon," I said. When the sermon was over, I took a few steps out before I blacked out. I couldn't even hear the 2,000-member congregation sing. When I awoke, I saw

돌아왔다. 정주 말이 "어머님, 우리는 어찌하려고 그러세요, 그만 하세요." 했다. 나는 "이제 겨우 시작인데……." 하고 딸을 위로했다.

영적 싸움은 매우 컸다. 실무자 총무는 모든 이사님들에게 협조를 못하게 거짓말을 퍼뜨리고 다녔다. 나는 그때 하나님 께서는 사람을 믿지 말고 오직 하나님만 믿으라고 하심을 확신하게 되었다. 은혜가 많은 곳에는 마귀의 장난도 많았다. 나를 가장 아껴 주시던 김성무 회장님은 교통사고로 돌아가셨고, 시회장으로 계시던 최금봉 회장님이 연합회 회장님이 되셨다. 건축 내용을 아무것도 모르시니 총무의 이야기만 들으시고 자꾸 나쁜 인상을 가지셨다. 한참 후 최 회장님은 내막을 파악하시고 매우 미안해하시며 나를 크게 위로해 주셨다. 나는 이 회관이 주님의 영광과 불쌍한 내 겨레를 위해 쓰여질 것을 생각하고 모든 고난을 참았다. 갖은 고난 끝에 우리 절제회 관은 아담한 석조 건물로 완성되었다. 이 모든 고난을 극복하게 한 성구를 소개한다.

"사랑은 오래 참고 사랑은 온유하며
시기하는 자가 되지 아니하며
사랑은 자랑하지 아니하며 교만하지 아니하며

Jung Joo crying next to me. I was carried to the nurse's room. After resting for a while, I later returned home. "Mother! What'll happen to us if you become ill? Please stop working!" Jung Joo spoke worriedly. "I have only just begun my work," I responded.

Everyone, including me, experienced much spiritual warfare at that time. The secretary of the KWCTU was tempted by the devil to spread lies among the trustees, causing the members to stop helping me. I was convinced that God wanted me to put my trust in Him alone, not in man. KWCTU President Sung Moo Kim suddenly died in a car accident, and Keum Bong Choi replaced her as the new KWCTU president. Not knowing anything about the construction affairs, and listening only to the secretary, Mrs. Keum Bong Choi's bad impressions of me grew with each day. It was only much later that she came to know the whole situation and felt apologetic. She comforted me a great deal. Convinced that the KWCTU Hall was to be built for the glory of God and for the benefit of the less fortunate, I endured the hardships that came my way. The KWCTU Hall was completed as a modest stone building. The following Bible passage helped me overcome my trials and tribulations:

⁴Love is patient, love is kind.

It does not envy, it does not boast, it is not proud.

⁵It is not rude, it is not self-seeking, it is not easily

무례히 행하지 아니하며 자기의 유익을 구하지 아니하며

성내지 아니하며 악한 것을 생각하지 아니하며

불의를 기뻐하지 아니하며 진리와 함께 기뻐하고

모든 것을 참으며 모든 것을 믿으며

모든 것을 바라며 모든 것을 견디느니라.”

(고린도전서 13장 4절-7절)

angered, it keeps no record of wrongs.
⁶Love does not delight in evil but rejoices with the truth.
⁷It always protects, always trusts,
always hopes, always perseveres.
(1 Corinthians 13:4-7)

5. 대한기독교여자절제회연합회 회장으로

"그런즉 너희는 먼저 그 나라와 그 의를 구하라.

그리하면 이 모든 것을 너희에게 더하시리라."

(마태복음 6:33)

"너희는 구제할 때에 오른손이 하는 것을 왼손이 모르게 하라."

(마태복음 6:3)

이 말씀을 몸소 실천하시며 평생을 사신 어머님을 본받아, 나는 선한 일은 기뻐하면서도 명예를 구하는 것을 경계했다. 대구에서 내가 절제회관을 봉헌할 때에도, 회장을 시킨다면 절제회 이사도 하지 않겠다고 미리 언질을 놓고 그 일을 마쳤다. 서울에서 절제회관을 구입하고 건축할 때에도 같은 심정이어서, 절제회 연합회 이사로서 건축 위원장을 맡으면서도 보이지 않는 곳에서 모든 일을 완수했다. 수많은 어려움 가운데서 절제회관 건축을 완성하도록 기적을 베풀어주신 주님께 감사드릴 뿐이다. 건축 완공 당시 절제회 연합회 회장이 되셨던 매넁숙 상도님은 일마 후 나를 방문하고 추임 절게회 연합회 회장으로 내가 절제회를 이끌어 달라고 간곡히 부탁을 하셨다. 내가 만약 그 책임을 맡지 않으면 절제회에 누를 끼칠

5. Elected President of the KWCTU

My mother had lived her life in obedience to these two Bible passages, and following her example, I also found joy in doing good works without seeking recognition. When I donated money towards the new KWCTU Hall in Daegu, I asked that the members not elect me as the KWCTU president, for otherwise I would refuse to serve as a trustee. I felt the same when the KWCTU Hall in Seoul was being constructed. I served as a trustee and as director of the KWCTU construction department, and I did not disclose the amount I donated. I only thanked the Lord that He manifested His miracles so that the KWCTU Hall could be completed in spite of all the difficulties. Elderwoman Young Sook Mae, national president of the KWCTU at the time of completion of the building, visited me one day and pleaded for me to accept the position as the next national president of the KWCTU. I found out that a certain person with personal intentions and agenda would take the position if I were to

사람이 그 역할을 하게 될 것이란 정황을 알게 되었다. 나는 고심 끝에 절제회 연합회 회장으로 추대하고자 하는 매영숙 장로님의 제안을 수락했다.

회장이 된 후 첫 사업으로 1972년 절제 장학사업을 시작했다. 1,000원, 3,000원씩 매달 적금으로 몇몇 절제 회원들의 협조를 얻어, 1976년부터 절제회가 결손가정을 도와서 자녀들에게 성적에 관계없이 교회에 적을 두고 있는 어려운 가정이면 누구든지 절제 장학생으로 선발하여 장학금을 지급했다. 장학 기금을 계속 증액하기 위하여 수년간 나는 매달 월급의 반은 장학 기금으로, 반은 선교비로 헌금하고 양말 한 컬레 사는 것을 아끼는 생활을 했다. 냉장고에 아침 식탁에 놓을 계란 10개만 있으면 감사하며 살았다. 장학금을 받는 학생들 가운데는 아버지가 세상을 떠났으나 장례비가 없는 가난한 가정도 있었고, 과부인 어머니와 함께 4형제가 서울역에 내릴 때 700원밖에 없었던 이도 있었다. 이러한 가정의 모든 자녀들이 절제 장학금을 받아 고등학교를 마치고 대학에 들어가서 훌륭한 신앙인이요, 사회의 일원으로 잘 자라고 있는 것을 보는 내 기쁨을 무엇에 비교할 것인가!

완성된 절제회관 건물에서 먼저 사창미연 방지사업을 했다. 무작정 시골에서 상경하는 소녀들을 모아 미용, 뜨개질,

decline, so I accepted Elderwoman Young Sook Mae's offer when she officially nominated me for the post.

The first project I launched as the national president was initiating a KWCTU scholarship fund with the help of KWCTU members. Beginning in 1972, the members were expected to give 1,000 to 3,000 won monthly for four years. Starting in 1976, we have been selecting candidates for KWCTU scholarships and giving bursaries to those who come from underprivileged families, strictly on the basis of need, not academic performance. For many years, in order to increase the scholarship fund, I had to live so frugally that at times I didn't even have enough money to buy a pair of socks for myself. I joyfully offered half of my monthly salary to the scholarship fund and the other half to the mission fund. I was thankful with just ten eggs in the refrigerator. Among the scholarship recipients, there was a student whose household was so poor that they couldn't even pay for his father's funeral. The mother of another student was a widow and she had only 700 won (equivalent to less than $1) in her pocket when she got off the train at Seoul Station with her four children. No words can explain the joy I feel whenever I see how these children have completed high school, graduated from university, and continue to mature as beautiful Christians and respectful members of society.

We used the new KWCTU Hall to shelter girls who had come from the countryside to Seoul with no definite objective in mind. We brought them from the train station and taught

양장을 본격적으로 가르쳐서 저들이 죄에 빠지지 않고 자립할 수 있게 돕는 애우관을 경영한 것이다. 얼마 후 시골 소녀들이 수출 산업을 위한 무역 공단의 전자 산업에 다 흡수되자, 현재 절제회관은 서울과 대구에서 절제 어린이집을 경영하여 어린이들에게 신앙과 절제 교육을 하면서 맞벌이 부부들의 일손을 덜어 주고 있다.

절제운동은 지난 70년간 전국 금주 금연 캠페인을 해 왔는데, 매년 연합회를 중심으로 술과 담배, 마약의 해독을 계몽하는 절제 팜플렛을 십만 장씩 찍어서 40여 지회를 통해 전국과 해외에 배포하고 있다. 서울역 캠페인은 한 해도 쉬지 않고 계속하고 있다. 신문, 방송, 텔레비전, 잡지 등 매스컴을 통해 금주 금연 운동을 펼쳐오고 있다. 나는 여성의 지위 향상에도 깊은 관심을 가지고 있다. 가족법 개정 위원회의 부회장으로 이태영 박사와 함께 18년간 꾸준히 노력하여 마침내 한국의 가족법 개정을 이루는 데 성공했다.

1980년부터는 3년마다 열리는 세계절제대회에 참석하게 되었다. 1983년 시카고에서 열린 세계기독교여자절제회 100주년 대회에서 서양화가인 큰딸 영주가 세계절제회 부회장으로 피선되었고, 1992년 스웨덴에서 열린 세계절제대회에서는 둘째 딸 김정주 박사가 세계절제회 부회장으로 피선되었다.

them how to be hairdressers, weavers, and dressmakers, lest they fall into sin and prostitution. We built a dorm in the yard and let the girls stay there, free of charge, until they were able to support themselves financially. When all the girls found jobs, thanks to Korea's rapidly growing electronic industries, the KWCTU in Seoul and Daegu started running childcare centers in order to take a load off the shoulders of working parents, teaching their children about temperance and instilling in their little ones the Christian faith.

The KWCTU has been campaigning against smoking and drinking for the last seventy years (up to 1993 when the memoir was first published. *Editor s note*). It publishes 100,000 pamphlets annually for distribution to its forty-some branches around the globe. The annual KWCTU campaigns at Seoul Station have continued all these years without ceasing since 1923, with the exception of some years during Japanese colonial rule and the Korean War. The KWCTU also continues to spread its campaigns through all available media, including newspapers, television, and magazines. I have always been interested in the advancement of the status of women in our society. For eighteen years I served as the vice president of the Committee for the Reformation of Family, and I helped reform family law in Korea.

Since 1980, I have been participating in the WWCTU's triennial world conventions and have had the opportunity to inform worldwide delegates of KWCTU's activities in Korea. In 1983 at the centennial of the WWCTU held in Chicago,

올리브 에드워드 세계기독교여자절제회 통신서기는 절제회 100년 역사상 한 어머니의 두 딸이 세계부회장으로 뽑힌 영광스러운 일을 처음 보았다고 내게 축하 편지를 보냈다.

절제회의 모든 사업은 그리스도의 복음을 증거하여 영혼을 구원하는 데 목적을 두고 있다. 그래서 나는 열심히 전도하여 구원 받은 영혼들과 다른 모든 절제회원들을 위해서 성경 공부를 지도하였다. 창세기, 이사야서 등의 말씀을 연구하면서 매달 성경 공부를 이끌었는데, 준비하면서 늘 내가 먼저 은혜를 받았다. 절제회 선교활동을 통해서 전도 받은 수많은 영혼들이 여러 교회에서 아름답게 헌신하는 것을 볼 때 가장 기쁘다.

절제회가 한국에 창립된 해와 나의 출생 연도가 다 같이 1923년임을 보며, 나는 하나님의 오묘하신 섭리를 깨닫는다. 신실하신 하나님 아버지께서 절제운동을 이 땅에 계속 발전하게 해주신 것을 감사드리며, 부족한 내게 절제운동의 귀한 사명을 맡기시고 성령의 능력을 부어 주셔서 그 사명을 잘 감당하게 하신 그 놀라우신 은혜를 찬양한다.

my eldest daughter, Young Joo, who is a painter, was elected World WCTU vice president and was reelected in Manila in 1986. And in 1992, Dr. Jung Joo Kim, my second daughter, was elected to the same post at the convention held in Sweden. Ms. Olive Edwards, world corresponding secretary of the WWCTU, sent a message congratulating me and saying that in the 100 years of WWCTU history, she had never seen two daughters of the same parents elected World WCTU vice president.

The work of the temperance movement seeks to inform humankind of the harms of alcohol, nicotine, and other addictive drugs and is focused on the spreading of the Gospel and the salvation of souls. I have diligently led Bible studies in order to save souls and nurture KWCTU members. I myself was greatly blessed by the Word of God when preparing Bible study lessons on the books of Genesis and Isaiah. I am most happy when I see those who have come to know Christ through the KWCTU actively serve the Lord in the church.

I see God's wonderful providence in seeing that I was born the very year the KWCTU was founded. Most of all, I am thankful that the Lord God our Father has always blessed the temperance movement, allowing it to carry on all these years. I give praise to the Lord for His amazing grace; for entrusting me, an unworthy servant, with a precious task; and for pouring His Holy Spirit upon me and guiding me every step of the way.

Chapter 3
Love is Enduring
— My Family
사랑은
온유하며

김영훈 회장 결혼
Wedding photos of Younghoon and Jung Yoon (1993)

70회 생신
On my 70th birthday (1993)

김영훈 회장 약혼식
Younghoon and
Jung Yoon's engagement
ceremony (1993)

에드워즈 (카나다)와
맑센 (덴마크) 대사 부부
With Ambassadors
Edwards of Canada and
Marxens of Denmark
(1993)

언더우드처럼 그리스도의
증인이 되려는 김영훈
회장의 세 자녀
Younghoon's
children who want
to witness Christ
(2003)

1. 사업가로 성공한 남편 김수근

나의 남편 김수근 대성그룹 창업회장은 1947년 5월 10일에 그의 회사를 창업했다. 직원이라고는 서기 김달홍 씨와 일꾼 한 사람뿐이었다. 대구 칠성동에 50평짜리 땅을 산 후, 맨 처음 그는 한 트럭 분의 석탄을 손으로 돌리는 기계로 찍어냈다. 이웃 회사 사장들은 그의 회사 규모가 작아서 아무도 그를 사장님이라고 하지 않고 이사님이라고 불렀다. 남편은 대학을 졸업하고 금융조합 이사로 근무한 적이 있어서 다른 사업가들에 비해 결코 능력이 부족하지 않았다. 그러나 금융조합 이사직을 정직하게 감당한 후여서 저축한 것이 없어 그 정도의 모욕은 감내해야 했다.

어느 날 남편은 내게 "아무래도 사업가 될 소질이 없나 봐." 하고 말했다. 이유를 물으니, 그는 "다른 이웃 회사 사장들은 다 술도 잘 마시고 노는데 돈을 많이 쓰는데, 나는 그렇게 하지 못하니 그렇다."라고 했다. 나는 그에게 말했다. "여보! 만약 술 잘 마시고 잘 노는 사람이 성공한다면, 한국 사람들이 전부 다 성공했게요. 그런 사람들은 추풍낙엽같이 다 떨어지게 될 것입니다. 오직 정직하고 부지런한 사람만이 하나님의 은혜 가운데 분명히 성공할 것입니다." 나는 담대한 믿음을 가지도록 그를 격려했다. 10년이 못 가서 술을 좋아했던 모

1. My Husband Soo Keun Kim, a Successful Businessman

My husband, Soo Keun Kim, founding chairman of the Daesung Group, started his business on May 10, 1947. He was the president of the company and had two employees: Mr. Dal Hong Kim, the clerk; and one laborer. Soo Keun bought a site that measured 50 *pyeong* (165 square meters) in the Chilseong-dong district in Daegu. In the beginning, the company bought only enough coal powder to fill one truck and made briquettes with a hand-operated machine. When the presidents of neighboring companies saw my husband's small business, they called him Director Kim instead of President Kim. But since my husband had a university degree and had worked as a director for several Farmers' Banks, he was as competent as they were. Nevertheless, he endured such ill treatment because he had no savings; he led an honest life, free of bribes and ill-gotten gains.

Soo Keun confessed to me one day, "I don't think I have what it takes to become a successful businessman." I asked him why he felt that way and he answered, "All the other company owners seem to maintain good business relations by drinking and partying together, and spending a lot of money, but I just can't afford that sort of lifestyle." So I replied, "Dear, if only those who drink and party succeed, then everyone in Korea would have become rich and successful by now. They will fall just like the leaves in autumn. God's grace and blessings fall on those who are diligent and upright.

든 사업가들은 고혈압과 간암으로 죽어, 그들의 부인들과 자녀들을 참으로 비참하게 만들었다.

얼마 후 남편의 친구 한씨가 사기를 쳐서 폐병으로 누워 있는 남편의 사촌인 김득림 씨에게 거짓말을 하고는, 그가 맡아 왔던 남편의 대동 연탄 주식을 다 가로채 갔다. 남편이 그의 사촌에게 달려갔을 때는 이미 늦었다. 그는 아픈 사촌이 불쌍하니 아무 말도 하지 못하고 사태가 그렇게 되어 참 민망하다는 말만 하고 돌아섰다. 집에 돌아 온 남편은 그의 전 재산을 다 잃음으로 인해 절망에 빠져 그만 몸져눕게 되었다.

그때 나는 하나님께 기도드리고 지혜의 말씀을 받았다. 나는 남편에게 말했다. "여보, 만약 당신이 사기로 재산을 다 잃어버려서 병들면 마귀만 좋아할 거예요. 돈은 벌 수 있지만, 건강은 한번 잃으면 쉽게 회복할 수 없으니까요. 그러니 이렇게 생각해 보세요. 어제 저녁에 도둑이 들어와서 당신의 모든 돈을 가져갔다고 생각해 보세요. 그렇다면 그렇게 마음이 상하겠어요? 오히려 '우리보다 더 가난한 사람이 우리 것을 조금 가져갔구나.' 하고 불쌍히 여기겠지요." 나의 말에 남편은 곧 바로 충격을 이기고 건강을 회복하여 기쁜 마음으로 자리에서 일어났다.

이 일이 있은 직후 우리 사촌 김득림 씨 집에는 하나님의

God will make the way for you and you will succeed by His guidance." I encouraged Soo Keun to walk boldly in faith. Within the next ten years, all the businessmen who had enjoyed the life of drinking and partying died from high blood pressure and liver cancer, leaving behind their precious wives and children in a state of great misery.

Some time later, a friend of my husband deceived Soo Keun's cousin Deuk Lim Kim, who was managing my husband's stocks in Dae Dong Co., Ltd., and fraudulently stole all of my husband's stocks. Cousin Deuk Lim was bedridden with tuberculosis at the time. By the time Soo Keun went to see his cousin, it was too late; there was nothing Cousin Deuk Lim could do to reverse the loss. Seeing his ill cousin, Soo Keun felt compassion towards him and so walked away without putting up a fight. He returned home feeling very sad about the whole situation. For a long time Soo Keun despaired over the loss of his entire fortune, and he eventually became very ill.

"Honey," I addressed Soo Keun one day after I prayed to God and received His words of wisdom, "if you remain sick because our fortune was stolen, you will bring greatest delight to no one but the devil. You can always earn more money; but once you lose your health, it's nearly impossible to recover. If a thief had broken into our house and had taken all our money, would you be as disheartened as you are right now? No, you would've had pity on the robber, for you would've

큰 기적이 일어났다. 그의 부모는 절에서 기도하여 아들을 얻었다고 하며 열심히 불교를 믿고 있었다. 결혼 후 나는 이 가족들이 예수님을 믿고 구원 받도록 부지런히 기도해왔다. 바로 이 사촌, 김득림 씨가 그 사기 사건 이후 어느 날 밤 매우 의미심장한 꿈을 꾸었다. 꿈에 그의 친구 하나가 와서 돈 보따리를 그에게 맡기고 떠났다. 한참 기다려도 친구가 오지 않자, 그는 그 돈을 다 써 버렸다. 그러나 그 친구가 다시 나타나서 돈을 달라고 했다. 그가 다 써버렸다고 대답하자, 그의 친구는 섭섭하다고 말하고 그를 떠났다. 바로 그때 예수님께서 오셔서 그가 매우 잘못했다고 꾸짖으셨다. 이 사촌은 예수님께 자신의 죄를 회개하고 용서를 구했다.

이 꿈에서 깨자마자 그는 부인에게 성경과 찬송을 사오라고 부탁했다. 그리고 또 목사님을 모시고 와서 예배를 드리고 싶다고 했다. 이 기쁜 소식을 듣고 나는 곧장 이상근 목사님과 심방하여 예배를 드렸다. 예배 중에 그는 성령의 은혜를 크게 받았다. 그날부터 그는 병상에서 그의 부모와 온 가족들을 전도하기 시작했다. 그의 부모님은 매우 완고하여, 예수님을 오히려 조롱했다. 그의 아들이 열심히 "그리스도를 믿으라."고 전도하자, 그의 아버지는 "만약 네가 나으면 나도 예수님을 믿으마." 하고 대답했다. 그러자 그 아들은 아버지를 꾸짖으면서

thought the robber must have needed the money that much." With these words, Soo Keun received new strength, a renewed spirit, and quickly recovered.

Soon after this incident, a great miracle happened in Cousin Deuk Lim's household. His parents were devout Buddhists. They had become followers of the Buddha when they conceived a son after many prayers at a temple. After I married into the Kim Family, I prayed diligently for Soo Keun's relatives and for their salvation. Cousin Deuk Lim had a dream a couple of nights after he was cheated of his wealth. In his dream, one of his friends entrusted him with some money and then left. Although Cousin Deuk Lim waited a long time, his friend didn't come back for the money, so he spent all of his friend's money. Just then, his friend returned and asked Cousin Deuk Lim to return the money to him. When Cousin Deuk Lim said he had spent it all, his friend turned away in disappointment. At that moment, Jesus came and rebuked him for his wrongdoing. Cousin Deuk Lim repented of his past sins and asked Jesus to forgive him.

As soon as he woke up from this dream, Cousin Deuk Lim asked his wife to buy him a Bible and a hymnal. He also said he wished to invite a pastor to their home and have a worship service. When I heard the good news, Reverend Sang Keun Lee and I visited this bedridden cousin. During the worship service, our cousin was greatly moved by the Holy Spirit and,

말했다. "아버지, 사람이 한 번 태어나 아파서 죽는 것은 자연스러운 일입니다. 내가 나아야지만 예수님을 믿겠다는 생각은 틀린 것입니다." 얼마 후 그의 부모와 자녀들은 모두 예수님을 믿게 되었다. 할렐루야!

우리는 우리의 전 재산을 잃었을 때, 그 아픈 사촌이 불쌍해서 한마디도 싫은 소리를 하지 않았다. 우리가 겉으로는 손해 본 것 같았지만, 주님께서는 그 온 가족들이 예수님을 믿도록 인도하심으로 진정한 이득을 얻게 하셨다. 성경의 가르치심은 참으로 진실하다.

"노하기를 더디 하는 자는 용사보다 낫고
자기의 마음을 다스리는 자는
성을 빼앗는 자보다 나으니라."(잠언 16:32)

만약 내가 하나님보다 돈을 더 사랑하였더라면, 근시안적으로 이 사촌에게 매우 화를 냈을 것이다. 그랬더라면 어떻게 이 가족들이 모두 구원받을 수 있었겠는가? 나는 물질에 욕심이 없도록 은혜를 베풀어주신 주님께 감사를 드렸다. 남편은 그의 사촌 가정에 일어난 소식을 듣더니 새 힘을 얻어 더욱 열심히 일했다.

on that day, he began to witness about Christ to his parents and his family from his bed. His parents were so stubborn that not only did they refuse to believe but they also mocked the name of Jesus. When Cousin Deuk Lim said to his parents, "Believe in Jesus," his father replied, "If you get well, I'll believe in Him." And to his father's response Cousin Deuk Lim said, "Father, it is natural for humans to die of an illness. It is wrong to say that you will believe in Jesus only if I get well." Eventually, his parents and his children all became Christians. *Hallelujah!*

Though we had lost a great deal, we did not say a word to our bedridden cousin. At first glance, it may appear as though we had lost a great deal, because we lost everything we owned, but in reality, the Lord blessed us with a great harvest by leading Cousin Deuk Lim's whole family to Jesus. How true is the Word of God!

> [32]*Better a patient man than a warrior,*
> *a man who controls his temper*
> *than one who takes a city. (Proverbs 16:32)*

If I had loved money more than God and had become short-sighted, I might have become very angry with Cousin Deuk Lim. But if I had, how would his family have learned of salvation in Christ? I thank God for His grace that kept my heart free from greed and materialism. When Soo Keun heard

　남편은 얼마 가지 않아 조선연료라는 큰 회사를 인수하기 위한 계약을 할 만큼 완전히 재기했다. 바로 그 때, 그의 친구 중에 고우일이라는 사람이 이른 아침에 방문했다. 나는 왜 그가 방문했는지 물었다. 남편은 그 친구가 사업차 급하게 돈을 빌리러 왔다고 했다. 나는 남편에게 곧 회사를 살 돈이니 빌려주지 말라고 충고했다. 내 눈에도 그의 친구 사업은 이미 파산된 것으로 보였다. 그럼에도 불구하고 계속 간청하는데 못 이겨 남편은 모은 돈을 다 빌려주었다. 그의 친구는 돈을 빌려갔으나, 사업이 실패하여 충격으로 곧 세상을 떠나고 말았다. 남편의 사업은 한동안 자본이 없어 심각한 타격을 받았다. 그럼에도 불구하고 그의 신용을 신뢰한 은행이 대출하여 줌으로써, 그는 조선연료 회사를 살 수 있게 되었다.

　얼마 후 세상을 떠난 친구의 부인과 아이가 우리 집을 방문했다. 나는 그 부인이 너무 불쌍해서 그에게 한마디도 할 수 없었다. 후에 그 부인이 보험외판원이 되었을 때, 남편의 회사 직원들이 다 고객이 되어 주었다. 그 부인은 그로 인해 자녀 교육을 시키고 집도 짓고 잘 살게 되었다. 나는 그 부인에게 돈에 대하여 아무 말도 하지 않도록 은혜를 주신 주님께 진심으로 감사드린다.

　남편은 태백산에 광산을 사고 그곳에 교회를 지어 목사님

about the miracle that had happened in his cousin's household, he received new strength and worked even harder.

Before long, my husband's business recovered enough for him to consider acquiring a large company called Chosun Fuel Co., Ltd. One of Soo Keun's friends, Woo Il Koh, came to see him early one morning. Asking Soo Keun why his friend had come, I learned that his friend was in urgent need of money for his business. I advised my husband not to lend his friend any money since we needed it to acquire the new company. Even I could see that his friend's business had gone bankrupt. Nevertheless, Soo Keun, moved by the urgency in his friend's request, lent him the money. Unfortunately, his friend passed away from shock and stress over his failed business. My husband's business struggled because of lack of funds, but the bank, trusting Soo Keun's credibility, loaned him money to acquire Chosun Fuel Co., Ltd.

The wife and one of the children of Soo Keun's deceased friend visited our house one day. I could not find any words to comfort his wife. She later became an insurance agent and all of my husband's employees willingly became her customers. Because of their help, she was able to put her children through school and build a house as well. I sincerely thank God for His grace that allowed me to hold my tongue and not mention anything of the money we had lent to her husband.

My husband purchased a coal mine in the Taebaek

도 모셨다. 후에 문경의 광산도 샀다. 이 광산은 매우 문제가 많아 누구든지 손을 대면 실패했다고 한다. 다른 사업가들은 김수근 씨가 이때까지 운이 좋아 성공했지만 문경광산만큼은 실패할 것이라고 말했다. 그러나 부지런한 성품을 타고 난 남편은 "잘 되는 광산을 팔 사람이 어디 있겠나?" 하고 말했다. 이 광산을 사고 나서, 많은 돈을 투자해도 전혀 이익이 없으니 그는 오래 고전했다. 그 광산의 가장 아름다운 곳에 교회가 서 있다.

이때 남편은 그의 사업을 더 확장하기 위해서 서울로 갔다. 그는 모든 자본을 광산에 투자했기 때문에 빈손으로 서울에 갔다. 서울에는 그를 반겨 줄 사람이 아무도 없었다. 명동에 작은 사무실을 하나 임대하고 비서 한 사람을 채용했다. 여기서 그는 사업 기회를 오래 모색했다.

오랜 심사숙고 끝에 그는 왕십리에 6·25로 인하여 거의 파괴된 공장 하나를 사기로 결심했다. 그 공장의 전 주인은 빚이 너무 많아서 5,000평이 되는 공장을 팔아도 그의 빚을 다 갚고 나면 집 한 채도 사지 못할 형편이었다. 남편은 법률을 공부했었기에 그 공장을 사는 데 관계되는 모든 법적인 문제점을 연구하고, 공장을 살 때에는 그 전 주인에게 많은 호의를 베풀었다. 그러나 전 주인 밑에 있던 한 직원이 오랫동안 법률

Mountains, where later he built a church and invited a pastor to minister in that region. Soo Keun later bought another coal mine in Mungyeong. This mine was so troublesome that everyone who had bought it had failed. People said that my husband may have succeeded thus far out of good luck, but that he would surely fail this time. "Who would sell me a coal mine if it were doing well?" Soo Keun would say. He, indeed, went through hard times after he purchased the coal mine in Mungyeong because it, in spite of a major investment, yielded no profit. But now (meaning 1977, when the author wrote her memoirs. *Editor's note*), a church stands at the most beautiful spot near the coal mine.

Soo Keun went to Seoul to further expand his business. Since he had invested all his money in the coal mine, he went to Seoul nearly empty-handed. No one was there to welcome him. He rented a small office in Myeong-dong and employed one secretary. He spent his days at the office looking for new business opportunities.

After much consideration, Soo Keun decided to purchase a factory in Wangsimni that had undergone great loss in the Korean War. The previous owner was in so much debt that the money he would receive after selling the 5,000-*pyeong* (16,500 square meters) factory, and after paying off his debts, wouldn't be sufficient to buy a house. Since Soo Keun had studied law, he did extensive research regarding all legal matters concerning the acquirement. He finally purchased it

사무소에서 서기로 일했던 사람이었는데, 남편이 이 공장을 사서 잘 운영하자 계약상에 한 단어가 빠져 있다는 구실로 남편을 고소했다. 남편은 이 일로 수년간 고생했으나 마침내 대법원에서 승소했다. 한편 서울의 연탄 업계에서는 대구에서 올라온 큰 경쟁자가 나타났다고 생각하고 크게 웅성거렸다. 서울의 사업가들은 상당히 신사적이어서 겉으로는 남편을 관대하게 대해 주었다.

머지않아 문경광산도 성공적으로 발전하여 전성기에는 2,000명의 직원과 광부들이 일했다. 남편은 그곳에 현대식 주택, 학교, 그리고 병원까지 갖추었다. 하나님 은혜로 남편은 산림 사업을 위해 문경광산 곁에 있는 이씨 왕가의 마지막 재산인 주흘산을 샀다. 이 산의 아름다움은 빼어나 국립공원의 하나로 지정되었다. 나와 아들, 딸들은 이 주흘산에 기독교 대학과 세계선교센터를 지어, 그곳에서 주님의 사역자들을 훈련하게 되기를 소망하고 기도한다. 주님께서 그 뜻대로 하실 것이다.

남편은 에너지 분야로 계속 사업을 확장하여 프로판가스 공장, 석유 사업 그리고 서울도시가스와 대구도시가스를 인수했다. 그의 회사는 제조업에도 뛰어들어가 가스보일러, 여러 가지 자동차 부품, 화학 약품 등을 생산하고 있다. 직원은

at a very reasonable price. One of the previous employees had formerly worked as a clerk at a lawyer's office. In seeing the factory operate smoothly, this man fell envious, found a loophole in the contract my husband signed, and sued him. My poor husband suffered from headaches for several years because of this matter, but he finally won his case before the Supreme Court. Meanwhile, others in the coal mine business were rather disturbed because they felt that a major competitor had come from Daegu. They were gentlemen and were friendly to my husband, at least outwardly.

The coal mine in Mungyeong was successful and, at its peak, had over 2,000 employees. Soo Keun built modern houses, schools, and even a hospital. By God's grace and provision, Soo Keun was able to buy Mt. Juheul—the last remaining property of the royal family—for his lumber business. The mountain's outstanding beauty has won it recognition as Korea's most spectacular national park. I hope and pray with my sons and daughters that, God willing, we can build a Christian university and a world mission center at Mt. Juheul so that servants of the Lord can be trained there. May the will of the Lord be accomplished.

Soo Keun expanded his business into the fuel industry, acquiring propane and oil companies, and also city gas companies in Seoul and Daegu. His company also started manufacturing gas boilers, various car parts, and chemical products. It now employs over 5,000 employees. Soo Keun

5,000명이 넘었다. 남편은 매일 아침 6시에 일어난다. 나는 매일 아침 남편보다 먼저 일어나서 주님께서 그와 모든 가족들이 하나님 영광을 위해 살게 해 주시기를 기도드린다. 남편은 다른 약속이 없으면 꼭 집에서 점심식사를 하고, 식사 후 30분간 수면을 취한 후 다시 오후에 사무실에 나가서 일하는 습관을 계속 유지했다.

열심히 일하는 남편을 내조하면서 나는 더욱 절제 생활에 힘썼다. 그 일례로 항상 내 손으로 기운 속옷을 자녀들에게 입혀왔다. 그들도 내가 기워준 속옷 입기를 즐겼다. 나는 "너희가 기운 속옷을 입었다고 욕할 사람은 한 사람도 없다. 우리 주위에 아직도 이렇게 가난한 사람이 많은데, 우리는 돈을 아껴서 이웃을 돕자."고 말하면서 어렸을 때부터 돈을 절약하여 이웃을 돕는 훈련을 시켜왔다. 이는 저들이 절제하여 성장함으로써 하나님의 귀한 일꾼이 될 것으로 믿기 때문이다. 나는 연탄 한 장을 볼 때에도 목숨을 걸고 탄을 캐내는 광부들의 손길이 떠올라, 내게는 그것이 보석과 같이 귀해 보인다. 그리고 남편이 힘들여 번 돈임을 생각할 때 동전 10원이라도 헛되이 쓸 수 없음을 깨닫는다. 나는 하나님께서 지금까지 남편의 건강을 지키시고 그의 사업이 무에서 출발하여 지금과 같은 대기업으로 발전할 수 있도록 인도해 주심을 항상 감사드린다.

wakes up at six o'clock every morning. I wake up even earlier to pray to God that He will bless my husband and my family to give glory to Him. Unless he has a special appointment, my husband comes home for lunch every day and takes a 30-minute nap before going back to work in the afternoon.

I have made greater efforts to lead a temperate life in order to help my hardworking husband. I have always mended my children's underwear myself. I used to reassure them, "No one will make fun of you for wearing mended underwear," which they didn't seem to mind in the first place. "We ought to save money so that it may be used to help the countless people around us who struggle to survive." I trained my children since their early years to save their money and to help their neighbors. I believed that they would become even more precious servants of the Lord if they were to learn of ways to live a temperate life from childhood. Whenever I look at a briquette, I consider it a precious jewel because it reminds me of the hands of miners who risked their lives to dig up the coal. Likewise, when I think about how hard my husband works to earn money, I cannot spend even ten won (equivalent to a penny) carelessly. I always thank the Lord for His blessings in keeping my husband in good health and for allowing Soo Keun's business to prosper, especially considering he started from scratch and raised the business into a leading enterprise. Whenever I see my

남편이 그토록 부지런하게 일하는 것을 볼 때마다 나는 잠언의 한 말씀을 기억한다.

"네가 자기의 일에 능숙한 사람을 보았느냐?
이러한 사람은 왕 앞에 설 것이요.
천한 자 앞에 서지 아니하리라."
(잠언 22:29)

남편이 그토록 부지런하게 일하는 것을 볼 때마다 나는 잠언

husband work so diligently, I am reminded of a passage from the Bible:

[29]*Do you see a man skilled in his work?*
He will serve before kings;
he will not serve before obscure men.
(Proverbs 22:29)

2. 셋째 아들 영훈이와 십자가

사람들은 내게 자녀들을 잘 키운 비결을 궁금해한다. 그러나 그것은 전적으로 하나님의 은혜였다. 자녀 교육의 한 예로 나는 셋째 아들 영훈이의 이야기를 나누려고 한다. 영훈이는 어릴 때부터 퍽 지능이 뛰어났다. 경북대 사대 부속초등학교에 입학하던 날, 자모들과 이야기를 하고 서 있는데 어떤 어머니가 "댁의 아드님을 좀 보세요."해서 보니, 벌써 앞에 나가서 "팅클 팅클 리들 스타."하면서 독창을 하고 있었다.

그 후 영훈이는 반에서 1등 아니면 2등을 하고 초등학교 다닐 때 선생님께 어려운 질문을 많이 해서 담임 선생님들을 꽤 당황하게 만들었다. 영훈이는 초등학교 때부터 저녁 식사만 마치면 30분 이내에 잠자기 시작하여 다음날 새벽 3시에 일어나, 형들이 사둔 책들을 많이 읽었다. 그러다가 아침 5시만 되면 배가 고파서 일하는 아주머니들에게 밥을 달라고 하니, 일하는 아주머니들이 방문을 꼭 잠그고 잠을 잤다. 아침 식사 전에 학교 숙제를 마치고 등교 후엔 선생님의 질문을 혼자서 다 대답했다. 선생님 말씀이 공부를 하려면 영훈이와 같이 하라고 하시면서 늘 칭찬하셨다.

나의 자녀 교육 방침은 어릴 때는 마음껏 뛰놀게 하며 별로 공부를 하라고 하는 일이 없었다. 우리 아이들은 초등학교 저

2. My Third Son, Younghoon, and the Cross

People always seem to be curious about my parenting principles and what my secret of raising good children is. There is no secret. All is because of God's grace.

I will now share a few stories about my son Younghoon as an example. From early childhood, Younghoon showed signs of exceptional talent. I was talking with the other mothers on his first day at elementary school when one of them pointed to my son and said, "Look at your son!" Younghoon was singing "Twinkle, Twinkle, Little Star" in English in front of all his classmates.

Younghoon was always one of the top two students in his class all throughout elementary school. He often asked his teachers many difficult questions, leaving his teachers often at a loss for answers. In his elementary school years, Younghoon would go to sleep thirty minutes after dinner and wake up at three o'clock the next morning to read his older brothers' books. Hungry at around five o'clock in the morning, he would ask the housemaids to make him breakfast, but they would just shut their doors and continue to sleep in. He usually did his homework before breakfast, and at school, he was always the first to answer the teacher's questions. His teachers spoke highly of him and told other students to study hard like Younghoon.

학년 때는 보통이다가 5·6학년이 되면 스스로 깨달아서 공부해서 다 한 번씩 1등을 하곤 했다. 영훈이는 5학년이 되어도 별로 키가 크지 않아서, 내가 어릴 때 아버지께서 뱀장어를 많이 사주신 기억이 나서 뱀장어 10마리를 하루걸러 한 번씩 먹였더니 지금 키가 178cm나 되게 자랐다.

영훈이는 경기중학교에 입학하였다. 일학년 때 곧 반장이 되었고 글짓기 대회에서 장원을 했다. 담임 선생님은 영훈이를 퍽 사랑하셨다. 가정 방문을 오셔서 하시는 말씀이 "저는 경기중학교에서 수 년을 가르쳤지만, 아직 영훈이같이 지도력이 있는 학생을 보지 못했습니다." 하고 칭찬을 하셨다. 그분은 영훈이가 중학교 2학년 때 다른 학교로 전근을 가셨는데도 영훈이가 중학교 졸업을 할 때 기억하시고 축전을 보내 주셨다.

영훈이는 경기중고등학교 재학 중 성화회(경기 기독학생회) 회원으로 활약하며, 성경 공부를 열심히 하고 성경 말씀을 매우 사랑하여 늘 묵상했다. 서울대학에 들어가서도 경기 성화회 수양회에 참석하여 후배들을 말씀으로 지도하고 사랑해 주었다.

영훈이의 음성은 바리톤으로 참 아름답다. 경기고등학교에 다닐 때, 학교 음악회에서 독창자로 뽑혀서 독창을 했다. 내가

One of my principles of educating my children was to avoid pushing them to study too much at a young age. Instead I would allow them to run around and simply be children. My children didn't excel much in their academic studies until they entered the fifth and sixth grades, where by then they realized the need to study and studied diligently by choice. All my children have reached the top of the class at least once.

Younghoon wasn' t that tall, even when he was in the fifth grade. I remembered how in my childhood, my father bought eels for me to eat so that I would grow. So I bought ten eels to cook for Younghoon, and now he stands tall at 178cm (5' 10").

Younghoon was admitted to Kyunggi Middle School, a highly prestigious school. In his first year, he was elected class president and received the highest honor in a creative writing contest. His homeroom teacher loved him dearly and spoke highly of him: "In all my years teaching at Kyunggi Middle School, I've never seen a student with such strong leadership skills." Though the teacher was transferred to another school the next year, he still kept Younghoon in his heart and sent a telegram congratulating him on his graduation from middle school.

During his years at Kyunggi Middle School and High School, Younghoon was an active member of a Christian students' association called the Holy Fire Club. He studied the Bible diligently, always meditating on the Word of God. Even after he enrolled at Seoul National University, he

맹장 수술을 하고 입원해 있을 때, 영훈이가 내 침대 옆에 와서 찬송을 불러 주어 그 노래가 너무도 아름다워서 나는 아픈 것도 잊고 잠이 들곤 했다. 나는 영훈이가 부르는 찬양 소리를 들을 수 있는 것이 무척 행복했다. 영훈이는 가정 예배 때에 나에게 복음 성가를 많이 가르쳐 주어서, 나는 이 노래들을 부를 때 은혜와 감사와 기쁨이 넘친다. 나는 아직 어떤 음반에서도 영훈이와 같은 바리톤 음성을 들어보지 못했다.

하나님은 영훈이에게 많은 독서를 하게 하신다. 그리고 책을 읽으면 그 후에 어찌나 재미있게 동생들과 부모님께 이야기를 해 주는지, 꼭 우리가 그때 그 시대에 살아서 그 모든 사실을 보고 있는 것처럼 쉽게 이야기해 준다. 남편은 독서를 많이 하는 어른인데, 영훈이가 건넌방에서 형제들에게 이야기를 시작하면 빨리 가셔서 그 이야기를 재미있게 들으시곤 했다. 우리 집에는 서재가 큰데 남편이 사업하다가 분주하여 이전에 읽었던 책이라도 혹 참고할 일이 있으면 언제나 영훈이에게 물었다. 그러면 영훈이는 그 많은 책 중에서 그 책을 찾아내어 페이지까지 정확하게 찾아 아버지께 만족한 회답을 드리곤 했다.

영훈이가 서울법대를 졸업하고 군복무도 끝냈을 때, 미국의 많은 좋은 학교에서 입학 허가가 왔다. 영훈이는 미국 앤아

attended the Holy Fire Club's retreats, where he ministered to younger students about the Word of God.

Younghoon has a beautiful baritone voice. While attending Kyunggi Middle School, he was chosen to sing a solo at a school concert. When I was hospitalized for appendicitis, Younghoon sat by my bedside, singing hymns to me. He sang so beautifully that I was able to forget about the pain and get a good night's rest. I was truly happy to hear his beautiful voice sing praises to God. Whenever we had family worship service, Younghoon taught me many gospel songs. When I sing those songs, I experience God's exceeding grace and overflowing joy. I have yet to hear a baritone voice more beautiful than Younghoon's , professional singers included.

The Lord blessed Younghoon with a desire to read. Every time he read a book, he shared with the rest of the family what he had read in such an interesting way and with such ease that we felt as if we ourselves were characters of the story. Soo Keun, who was also well-read, always joined our sons whenever Younghoon told stories to his brothers. We have a big library in our house. Whenever my husband needed to find a reference book for his work, he would ask Younghoon for help. My son would not only pick out the right book among the many there, but also showed his father the exact pages where the information could be found.

After Younghoon finished both his studies at Seoul National University and his military service, he received admissions from several universities in the United States.

보에 있는 미시간대학으로 갔다. 미시간에서 영훈이는 국제법학과 경영학으로 석사를 받았다. 영훈이는 미시간에서 공부할 동안 한인 교회에 나가 청년회를 지도하면서, 많은 선후배들을 주님 앞으로 인도했다. 졸업 후 영훈이는 귀국해서 시티은행의 중역으로 2년간 일하면서 시티크로스라는 이름의 기독은행원회를 조직했다. 그 후 하버드에서 4년간 경제학과 신학을 공부하고 신학 석사(M.Div) 학위를 받았다.

영훈이가 하버드 대학교에서 공부할 때 일이다. 하버드 대학이 350주년을 맞이하여 중요한 행사의 하나로, 하버드의 신학 역사를 연구 발표하도록 조지 윌람스 교수에게 부탁했다. 이 교수는 하버드에서 바른 기독교인 한 사람을 발굴하여 이 작업을 함께 하고자 기독학생회 지도교수인 짐과 뷰라 쇼 교수 내외분께 기독학생회 회원들 가운데 한 사람을 추천해 주도록 부탁했다. 짐과 뷰라는 영훈이를 추천하였다. 영훈이는 처음에는 본인의 석사 논문 준비도 있고 해서 바쁘다고 사양했으나 그 교수님이 너무도 간곡히 부탁함으로 허락하여, 하버드의 역사 자료 도서실에서 50시간을 보내면서 하버드의 청교도저 신하의 기원과 변천 과정을 정리해 냈다. 조지 윌리암스 교수는 영훈이의 연구 결과를 토대로 350주년 하버드 역사를 발표하게 됨을 진심으로 감사했다.

Younghoon decided to go to the University of Michigan, at Ann Arbor, where he received a master of arts degree in comparative law and a master of business administration. While he was studying in Michigan, he was a young adults leader at a Korean church and helped many people meet Christ. After Younghoon returned to Korea, he worked at Citibank Seoul as an assistant manager for two years. There, together with other Christian bankers, he formed a Christian fellowship called the City Cross. Later, he studied International Economics at Harvard University Graduate School and then received a Master of Divinity at Harvard Divinity School.

When Younghoon studied at Harvard Divinity School, the university celebrated its 350th anniversary. Professor George Williams was requested to present on the theological history of Harvard University for the school's anniversary. Professor Williams wished to work on the project with a sincere Christian student. When he asked Professors Jim and Vera Shaw, faculty advisors to the Harvard-Radcliffe Christian Fellowship (HRCF), to recommend a member of HRCF to assist him with the project, they recommended Younghoon. At first, Younghoon declined because he was too occupied with writing his dissertation, but he finally gave in when Professor Williams insisted. After spending nearly fifty hours in the archives, Younghoon finished his research on the origins and transformation of Harvard University. Professor Williams was able to report on the history of Harvard at its 350th anniversary and he thanked Younghoon for his great

1987년 영훈이는 하버드대학교를 졸업했다. 하버드의 시작과 현재를 비교하는 그의 석사 논문에서 하버드가 '그리스도와 교회를 위해서' 시작했으나 지금은 그 창설자의 뜻과 멀리 떨어져 있음을 지적하고 학교 전체와 나아가서 미국 사회가 그 죄를 회개하고 그리스도 앞으로 돌아와야만 진정한 희망이 있음을 강조했다.

귀국 후 영훈이는 대성그룹에 입사하였다. 현재 대성그룹 회장으로서 그리스도의 말씀에 순종하며 기업을 경영하고 있다. 매일 영훈이는 모든 사업 영역의 올바른 결정을 위해 하나님의 지혜를 겸손하게 구하고 있다. 하나님께서는 영훈이에게 변치 않는 견고한 믿음과 겸손한 성품으로 축복해주셨다.

영훈이가 가장 사랑하는 두 신앙인이 있다. 첫 번째는 9세기에 영국을 통일하고 기독교 국가로 견고하게 만든 신학자요 장군이었던 알프레드 대왕이다. 두 번째는 "오직 예수 그리스도를 믿음으로서 우리가 하나님 앞에 의롭다 함을 받는다."는 진리의 횃불을 높이 들어 경건과 학문을 통해서 종교개혁을 완수한 칼빈 선생님이다. 이 두 신앙의 용사처럼 나는 영훈이가 하나님의 귀한 종으로 온전히 쓰임 받기를 매일 기도하고 있다.

영훈이는 1993년 11월 3일, 금란교회 김홍도 목사님의 둘

help in gathering all the necessary materials.

Younghoon graduated from Harvard Divinity School in 1987. In his dissertation, he compared the beginning and present spiritual state of Harvard. He pointed out that the university had wandered away from its founding vision, "for Christ and His Church"—*Christo et Ecclesiae* as written on its original seal in Latin. He emphasized that the only hope for the school and American society as a whole may lie in its repentance of sins and its return to Christ.

Upon return to Korea, Younghoon joined the Daesung Group. Even now, as chairman of the Group, he continues to work in obedience to the Word of God, seeking wisdom from God with a humble heart. God has blessed Younghoon with a good character and has allowed him to continue to walk strongly in faith.

There are two men of faith Younghoon respects most: King Alfred the Great, who was a warrior king and theologian that unified the Anglo–Saxons and turned his country into a strong Christian nation in the 9th century; and John Calvin, who in the 16th century brought about reformation in the church, in accordance with piety and science, by raising the banner of the Truth of the Gospel, and who proclaimed that we are justified only by faith in Jesus Christ. I pray daily that Younghoon may be used wonderfully just like these two bold soldiers of faith, according to the will of God.

Younghoon married Jung Yoon Kim, the second daughter

째 딸 김정윤 양과 결혼했다. 잠언 31:10~31에 나오는 현숙한 여인과 같은 아내를 맞이하고자 오래 드려왔던 기도가 응답되어 기뻤다. 김홍도 목사님은 교인이 20명밖에 없던 금란교회를 1970년도에 맡아 현재 10만여 명의 대교회로 부흥시킨 목사님이시다. 그 어머니 이숙례 전도사님은 네 아들(김선도, 김홍도, 김국도, 김건도)을 모두 목사님으로 만드신 귀한 주의 종이시다. 영훈이의 결혼식에는 6천여 명의 하객 분들이 오셔서 마치 부흥회와 같았다. 영훈이와 정윤이는 함께 기도하며 자녀들을 귀한 그리스도의 증인으로 바르게 키우고자 늘 힘쓰고 있다.

of Reverend Hong Do Kim, on November 6, 1993. I am glad that Younghoon's prayers to marry a woman of strength as outlined in Proverbs 31:10-31 has been answered. Reverend Hong Do Kim is a well-known pastor. He began serving Kumnan Methodist Church in 1970 when there were only twenty members in the congregation. Now his ministry has grown into a large church with over 100,000 registered members. Reverend Kim's mother, Evangelist Suk Rye Lee, is also a precious servant of the Lord who has raised all four of her sons to become pastors: Seon Do Kim, Hong Do Kim, Kuk Do Kim, Keon Do Kim. About 6,000 guests attended Younghoon's wedding. The ceremony looked like a big revival meeting. Younghoon and Jung Yoon always pray together that they may carry out their precious task of raising their God-given children to become witnesses for Christ.

나는 어릴 때 어머님께 한 번도 꾸지람을 받아 본 적이 없다. 항상 칭찬과 더불어 성경 말씀을 가르쳐 주셨다. 그래서 어머님과 길을 가다가 다른 아이가 길에서 맞는 것을 보면 저런 어머님은 무식해서 그런 줄만 알고 있었다. 그 후 나는 가끔 교양 있는 부모들도 아이들을 잘 꾸짖고 때리는 것을 보았다. 그럴 때마다 나는 어머님께 감사했다. 나도 어렸을 때 잘못을 많이 했을 터인데 어째서 나의 어머님은 한결같이 사랑하셨는지, 지금 생각하니 그것은 인간의 사랑이 아니라 예수님의 아가페 사랑임을 깨달았다.

나의 넷째 오빠가 신앙 생활이 좀 부족한 것을 보시고, 어머님은 그를 꾸짖지 않으시고 40일을 금식하고 기도하시는 것을 보았다. 그때 나는 큰 감동을 느꼈다. 나는 어머님께 여쭈었다. "어머님, 시장하시지 않으세요?" 어머님 대답이 "아가야! 3일만 넘으면 하나님의 힘을 얻어 아무렇지도 않단다."고 하셨다. 나는 어린 마음에도 존경과 함께 안타까운 생각이 들었고 지금도 가슴이 찡하다. 그 후 우리 오빠는 어머님의 금식기도에 일평생 감사하고 있다.

하루는 어머님이 임 사장님 댁을 방문하셨다. 그때 마침 저녁 무렵이라 임 사장님은 반가운 얼굴로 회사에서 퇴근을 하였는데, 그 부인은 짜증을 내면서 하루 종일 아이들이 자기를 애

3. My Mother's Advice

I was never reprimanded by my mother during my childhood. I only remember her giving me words of encouragement and teaching me about the Word of God. So whenever I saw a mother spanking her child on the street, I thought, *How ignorant she must be.* But then again, I even saw educated women yelling at and spanking their children. I thanked my mother every time I made such observations. Now that I think about it, my mother loved me not with humanly love but with Jesus' *agape.*

When my mother saw that my fourth brother was not walking with Jesus, she chose to fast forty days, rather than reprimand him. I was greatly moved. I asked her one day, "Aren't you hungry?" Mother replied, "As long as I get through the first three days, the power of God will fill me up and lead me through all the way." As a little girl, I was filled with much respect for my mother. Still, I am moved whenever I think back to this time. My brother remains grateful for mother's fasting and prayers.

My mother once told me about the time she witnessed to the Lim Family. Mr. Lim was in a happy mood when he returned home from work at dinner time, but when his wife told him all the ways their children had misbehaved that day, his smiling face gradually became stern and angry. My

먹인 이야기를 털어놓았다고 한다. 웃으면서 집에 돌아온 아빠의 얼굴은 자꾸 굳어져 갔다. 나중에는 성난 얼굴이 되었다. 어머님은 "아가야, 너는 다음에 결혼하거든 이런 어리석은 여성이 되지 말아라. 하루 종일 남자가 밖에 가서 사업하느라 시달리고 오는데, 집에 있던 아내는 종일 아이들의 귀여운 것만 생각해 두었다가 남편에게 이야기하렴. 그러면 그 남편이 얼마나 즐거우며, 하루의 피로가 다 회복되지 않겠니?" 나는 어머님의 가르침을 순종하여 남편이 퇴근할 때는 반드시 좋은 일만 생각해 두었다. 아름다운 아이들의 재롱이나 잘한 일만 얘기하면 온 종일 피곤했던 남편의 몸이 풀리고 기분이 전환됨을 역력히 볼 수 있었다.

나는 이 모든 어머님의 교훈을 일생 동안 마음에 새기면서 아이들을 기를 때에도 절대 꾸짖지 않았다. 아이들이 잘못할 때 옆에 잘한 형제를 칭찬하면, 저도 칭찬을 받고 싶어서 노력하는 것을 자주 보았다. 학교에서 시험 성적이 나빠도 나는, "애야, 너 시험에서 틀린 것을 잘 알았니?" 하고 묻기만 한다. 아이들이 "네!" 하고 대답하면 나는 "그러면 더 잘 됐어. 오늘 잘 알지 못하고 쓴 것이 맞았으면 이 다음에 중요한 시험 때 틀리기 쉽지만, 엄마도 시험에 한 번 틀렸던 것은 오래오래 기억에 남아서 더 잘 알게 됐어. 괜찮아!" 그리고 나면 아이들은 사기가 죽지 않고 더욱 분발하는 것을 체험했다. 아이들이 위로

mother advised me: "My dear child, when you get married, don't become like this foolish woman. Our husbands work all day and they come home completely exhausted. While at home, think of all the good times you shared with your children during the day to tell your husband. Don't bring his spirits down with bad news. Don't you think then that your husband will be happy and find rest?" I try to follow her instructions; I try to remember all the good things that happen each day so that I can share them with Soo Keun, and I see how he is able to forget about all the stresses of the day and finally relax when he hears good news about our children.

When raising my children, I followed the example of my mother's instructions and have never reprimanded my children. Whenever they misbehaved, I would compliment another child. And when that child saw another sibling get attention, he or she would correct himself or herself to receive praise too. When they received a low grade on their exams, I asked them, "Do you know why you got that question wrong?" And if they answered yes, I would say: "That's good, for if you got the correct answer by guessing, you are sure to make bigger mistakes when it comes to important exams. Since you got the question wrong, you'd better remember what to do and what not to do next time. It's okay!" My children were encouraged to put more effort into their studies. The whole purpose of raising children is to give

하나님께 영광이 되고 우리 가정의 기쁨이 되며 국가 사회의 좋은 인물로 성장해가게 하는 것이 목적인데, 학교 성적을 좋게 하려고 심하게 다그치고 과외에 신경을 많이 쓰는 것은 좀 생각해 볼일이다.

나는 어머님이 주신 많은 교훈 가운데 가정을 아름답게 이끌려면 하나님의 법도인 성경 말씀을 많이 봉독하면서 그 말씀대로 살아야 함을 깨닫고 실천했다. 그러면 가정에 항상 사랑이 넘치면서 평화롭고 성품이 좋은 자녀들을 기를 수 있다. 나의 어머님께서는 험한 인생 길을 잘 살 수 있는 법도를 성경적으로 가르쳐 주셨다. 나는 가정 생활의 성공을 첫째, 하나님께 감사 드리고 어머님이 신앙 가운데서 지혜로운 여성이 될 수 있도록 진리의 교훈을 주심을 항상 감사하고 있다. 내가 세상을 떠날 때, 내 자녀가 아름다운 추억을 가지게 되도록 항상 노력한다. 제일 좋은 가정 교육법은 매일 가정 예배를 드리는 일이다. 매일 하나님께 가정 예배를 드리는 가정의 자녀는 이 사회와 국가의 유용한 인물이 될 줄로 확신한다. 우리는 모두 연약한 인생이지만 매일 가정 예배를 통해 기도하고 서로를 사랑하면서 천국을 경험할 수 있다. 이런 가정에는 절대로 문제아가 나지 않는다. 오히려 남에게 모범이 되는 자녀가 자라고 하나님의 축복이 차고 넘친다.

glory to God in the highest, to share the joys of life with each other, and to help them contribute to society. Perhaps there is a need for parents to reconsider how much emphasis they put on their children's academic performance.

At the heart of my mother's lessons and advice, I have found the need to meditate upon and live according to God's Word. In doing so, our homes will be filled with love and harmony, and parents will raise godly, peaceful children. My mother taught me how, in accordance with the Bible, we can live well despite unfavorable situations. I give thanks to God for giving me a wise mother and for the beautiful family He has helped me raise. My mother always taught me in her faith and in the light of the Bible so that I would become a woman who always seeks God's wisdom. I too have put much effort into my parenting principles so that when I leave this world, my children may have beautiful memories of me. The most important and effective parenting principle is to have family worship service daily. I am confident that children of such families will contribute greatly to society and our nation. Though we are weak human beings, if we grow in a godly family, worshipping the Lord daily and loving one another, we will be able to enjoy heaven on earth. Our households will prosper; our children will develop into exemplary individuals; and God's blessings will overflow.

4. 자녀 교육에 필요한 세 가지 양육 방법

　우리 자녀들을 아름답게 키워 주신 하나님의 은혜를 묵상해 본다. 귀한 생명을 주신 하나님께서 이들이 아름답게 열매 맺도록 하심에 아래의 세 가지 방법으로 역사하셨음을 회상하며 모든 젊은 여성들과 부모들에게 도움이 되고자 기록해 본다.

　첫째, 태교의 역할이다. 아기가 태 중에 있을 때 나는 일체 잡지나 신문들을 보지 아니하고 오직 성경 말씀만을 보며 열 달을 지냈다. 아기를 위해서 하나님께 기도하며 열 달을 지내고 아기를 낳으니, 아기들은 모태에서 성령으로 충만함을 받아 착하게 자란다.

　둘째, 성경 말씀 교육이다. 젖 먹일 때부터 무릎에 올려놓고 다윗과 골리앗, 에스더, 요셉, 모세, 예수님의 생애를 이야기해 주었다. 그러다 보면 유년 주일학교에 들어가기도 전에 벌써 아이들은 신구약 이야기를 익히 알게 되고 하나님의 말씀을 사랑한다. 날마다 저녁에 온 가족이 모여서 가정 예배를 드리면서 가족들이 가장 기뻐하고 즐거워하는 시간을 찬양과 말씀과 기도의 시간으로 삼는다.

　셋째, 유년 주일학교 생활이다. 학교에 입학하기 전에 교회에 나가면, 유년 주일학교에서 말씀과 찬양과 기도를 배운다. 그리고 교회 친구들과 성도의 교제를 하며 교회 안에서 꽃과

4. Three Spiritual Foods for Children

I stand in awe of God's grace, which has allowed my children to grow beautifully. God granted me the wisdom necessary to raise my children, my most precious gifts from God, to bear much fruit. I hope the following advice may be of help to all the mothers and young parents out there.

First, do not overlook prenatal care. For the entire nine months that I was pregnant, I only read the Bible. I never once glanced at newspapers or magazines. I also prayed for my babies during pregnancy, and I believe that is why they were filled with the Holy Spirit from birth and were born with good character.

Second, teach your children about the Bible. When nursing my children, I held them in my arms and told them about Jesus and the stories about Joseph, Moses, David and Goliath, and Esther. That way, your children are familiar with the Bible even before they are old enough to go to Sunday school. It instills in them a love for Christ and for the Word of God. Every evening, gather the family to share a blessed time of praise and worship, meditation upon the Scriptures, and prayer.

Third, send your children to Sunday school. By enrolling them in Sunday school even before they enter kindergarten, your children will learn about the Word of God, how to sing

같이 아름답게 자라난다.

　이렇게 아름다운 세 가지의 영양을 먹고 자라나는 아이들은 학교에 들어가서, 이미 형성된 훌륭한 인격의 바탕 위에 지식을 배워간다. 학교 교육은 마치 아름다운 바탕으로 훌륭하게 짠 천에 수를 곱게 놓는 작업과 같이 순조로운 것이 된다. 우리에게 지혜와 믿음을 주셔서 만세 반석이신 그리스도 위에 인격의 집을 짓도록 인도해 주신 하나님께 세세토록 영광을 돌릴지어다. 아-멘.

praises to the Lord, and how to pray. Also, through fellowship with other children and members of the church, your children will surely bloom beautifully like flowers.

Children who grow with these three spiritual foods develop good character, even before they enter school, on top of which they can accumulate and acquire knowledge at school. The knowledge children acquire at school can be likened to the intricate embroidery that is sewn on well-made fabric—the latter being made carefully of the three spiritual foods. May all glory be to God, Who, by giving us wisdom and faith, has made it possible for us to build a house of character upon the everlasting rock that is Christ. Amen.

Chapter 4

The Word of the Lord is a Lamp to My Feet

주의 말씀은 내 발에 등이요

김영훈 회장 성지순례
Younghoon`s pilgrimage to the
Holy Land (1979)

28회 절제총회 설교
Delivering a sermon at the 28th
KWCTU Convention (1991)

고희 예배
My 70th birthday
thanksgiving service
(May 10, 1993)

1982년 여성단체협의회 용신봉사상 수상
After receiving the Korean National Council of
Women Award for Distinguished Public Service (1982)

1978년 12월 세계선교기금 모금을 위한 절제회 자선패션쇼
At the KWCTU Charity Fashion Show to raise world
missions funds (December 1978)

1989년 6월 데이비드 애드니 선교사님 초대로 캘리포니아
데이비스시 중국교회 설교 후
Invited by Missionary David Adeny to preach at a
Chinese church in Davis, California (June 1989)

1. 회개

　　우리 인간은 아담의 죄를 유전 받고 이 세상에 태어났다. 그러므로 성경은 "의인은 없나니 한 사람도 없다."고 분명히 말씀하셨다. 죄라는 것은 몸의 암과도 같다. 수술을 해야만 완전하다. 이 세상에 흔히 안 믿는 사람들은 자기들에게는 죄가 없다고 생각한다. 나도 과거에는 그렇게 생각했다. 우리가 방을 청소하고 앉아 있으면 이 방에는 먼지가 없다고 생각한다. 그러나 햇빛이 그 방에 들어오면 수많은 먼지를 볼 수 있다. 우리가 아직 광명하신 하나님의 빛에 속하지 않고 어두운 세상의 악령에 속하여 있으면, 자기는 아무 죄가 없다고 생각하며 또 죄를 지어도 큰 양심의 가책이 없다. 남이 안 보면 죄가 아닌 줄 안다. 이렇게 하여 인생은 죄 가운데 태어났다가 죄 가운데 죽어 간다. 예수님 말씀에 "너희가 물과 성령으로 거듭나지 않으면 하나님 나라에 들어갈 수 없다."라고 하셨다. 우리의 과거의 모든 죄가 예수님의 보혈로 용서함을 받고 우리가 성령으로 다시 태어나지 않으면 하나님 나라에 들어갈 수 없다. 하나님은 빛이시며 어두움이 조금도 없으신 신이심으로, 우리는 죄의 몸을 가지고는 하나님의 자녀가 될 수 없다. 우리 인생에게 양심이란 것을 주셨건만, 연약한 인생인지라 죄를 지을 수밖에 없다. 그러나 하나님께 참으로 회개할 때 우

1. Repentance

At birth we are born with the inheritance of the original sin of Adam. The Bible says, "There is no one righteous, not even one." (Romans 3:10) Sins are to the soul as cancer cells are to the body—they must be removed, that is, through spiritual cleansing. Many non-Christians are led to believe that they are without sin. I too was one. Suppose you cleaned your room. You sit down and look around yet do not see a speck of dust. But when sunlight enters the room, we can see that the entire room is filled with dust. In this way, when we are away from the light of God and continue to roam about in darkness, we are bound to believe we are free of sin or even become devoid of any guilty conscience. It is easy to believe that if others cannot see the sins we commit, we are not with sin. Man is born, however, with sin and dies with sin.

[5]Jesus answered, "I tell you the truth,
no one can enter the kingdom of God
unless he is born of water and the Spirit."
(John 3:5)

All our sins can be washed away by the blood of Christ. If we aren't born again through the Holy Spirit, we cannot enter the Kingdom of God. God is Light; there is no darkness in

리 하나님은 긍휼을 베푸사 용서하신다.

그러나 흔히 많은 사람들은 자기가 죄를 지어도, 하나님은 사랑이 많으시니 무조건 용서하실 줄 아는데, 이것은 큰 오해다. 알지 못하고 죄를 지을 때는 회개하면 용서가 성립되지만 고의로 죄를 짓는 자들에게는 만일 신속하게 진심으로 회개하지 않으면 하나님의 무서운 심판이 기다리고 있음을 우리는 알아야 된다. 예를 들면 모든 죄는 몸 밖에 있지만 간음죄는 몸 안에 있는 죄이다. 하나님은 불꽃같은 눈으로 심판의 채찍을 들고 계신다.

한 시라도 빨리 죄에서 떠나는 자는 그만큼 더 행복할 수 있다. 그의 생은 의미 있는 삶이 된다. 인생은 그 생명이 풀의 꽃과 같다. 이 짧은 생을 좀더 가치 있게 살려고 하면 속히 하나님께 모든 죄를 회개하여야 한다. 그렇게 하면 하나님은 의로우신 분이라서 우리에게 큰 은혜를 베푸신다. 이 축복을 많은 사람들이 받으시기를 축원한다.

Him. And so we cannot call ourselves children of the Light if we are with sin. Although God gave us a conscience, we are weak and still commit sins, but when we repent before God with a truthful heart, God will be merciful and forgive us.

All too often, people commit sins and do not doubt for a moment that God will forgive, but they are being deceived. When one repents for committing a sin, God forgives, but if we intentionally sin, unless we truly repent, we must recognize that we will face God's judgment. Sin is usually committed outside the body, but the source and residue of sin remain within the body. God dispenses judgment with a fierce blazing in His eyes.

The earlier you repent, the more joy you can experience in your lifetime, and you will have a greater purpose in life. Those who wish to live a more purposeful life must repent of their sins, and God, Who is just and true, will shower down grace upon them. It is my wish that crowds of people may receive His blessings.

2. 평화와 기쁨

나는 일생 동안 기쁘고 또 기쁜 생활의 연속이었다. 시집와서 아직 남편이 학생일 때 심히 궁핍하였고 설상가상으로 시어머님도 병환으로 계셨지만 내 마음속에는 항상 기쁨이 샘솟았다. 내 입에는 기쁨의 찬양이 끊이지 않았다. 아이들을 기를 때 항상 찬송과 기도가 내 입에서 떠나지 않았다. 모두 하나님의 평화의 선물이었다. 하나님을 진정으로 사모하는 사람은 누구나 이러한 은혜를 받는다. 이 은사는 예수님을 참 구주로 모시고 믿어 보지 않은 사람은 모른다. 예수님 안에만 하나님이 주시는 참된 평화가 있다. 이 참된 평화를 가진 자는 어떤 처지에서도 만족하고 감사하는 생활을 할 수 있다. 이것이 믿는 자의 특권이다.

내가 많은 은혜를 베푼 자가 나를 배신 할 때도 "사랑은 오래 참고"라는 성경 말씀을 의지하면 승리할 수 있다. 또 마음에 번민이 있어서 잠이 오지 않을 때에도 찬양을 부르면, 하늘로서 내리는 평화가 강같이 흘러 항상 단잠을 이룰 수가 있다. 해가 지도록 분을 품지 말라는 말씀을 실천해보면 이 말씀은 하나님이 자기 자녀를 사랑하셔서 주신 말씀인 것을 깨달을 수 있다. 나는 병들었을 때에도 평화가 하늘 문을 열고 폭포수와 같이 내려옴을 체험했다. 우리 민족과 나아가서 모든 인류가 예수 그리스도를 믿고 이 평화와 기쁨을 소유하시기를 기도드린다. (1977년 성탄절 절제회 설교 중)

2. Peace and Joy

(KWCTU Christmas sermon, 1977)

I have experienced unending joy throughout my life. Though we were poor early on in our marriage life, as Soo Keun was still a student, and though I faced the added stress of caring for my bedridden mother-in-law, waterfalls of joy always overflowed in my heart. Joyful hymns were always on my lips. When I raised my children, words of praise and prayer never left my mouth. All who have a heart for God can receive His grace. This gift is invisible to those who have yet to receive Christ as their Savior, for God's perfect peace is received only through faith in Christ. All who have this gift of peace in their hearts experience pure joy and thanksgiving, regardless of changing conditions. And this is the special privilege that all who believe in Him have.

When I showed kindness but was betrayed and rejected, I meditated upon the Scripture about how love is patient and I claimed victory. And when I agonized over a matter and couldn't fall asleep, I sang hymns and, feeling peace from heaven flow over me like a river, I was able to enjoy a sweet, sweet sleep. Now I understand that God called us to settle matters before the sun goes down. Because He loves us, He wants us to receive His gift of perfect peace. Even when I was ill, I experienced a release from worry and felt peace flow through me from the gates of Heaven. I pray that our nation, and all nations in this world, may believe in Christ and experience the peace and joy of God.

3. 감사하며 사는 생활

인생에게는 크게 나누어 두 가지 타입이 있다. 감사하며 사는 사람과 불평하며 사는 사람이 있다. 초가삼간에 살면서도 감사하는 사람이 있는가 하면 높고 부유한 집에서도 불평과 불만이 가득한 사람이 있다. 그러나 적은 것을 받고도 그 은혜를 일생 잊지 않고 기억하고 감사하는 사람도 있다.

예수님을 나의 구주로 모시는 사람은 누구나 다 이 감사생활을 할 수 있다. 우물처럼 솟아나는 이 감사는 억제할 길이 없다. 나는 가난할 때도 감사하는 마음이 매일 우물처럼 솟아올랐다. 나의 어머님은 병고로 6년을 사시면서 하루에도 몇 차례씩 감사 하셨다. 교인들이 위로하러 오셨다가 병중에 계신 분이 깊이 감사하시니 도리어 은혜를 받고 가셨다. 나는 매일 아침 하나님께 지난밤 평안한 안식을 주심에, 오늘 또 기동할 수 있는 생명을 주심에 대해 감사 드렸다. 나의 감사 조건을 몇 가지 적어 보려 한다.

1. 예수님을 나의 구주로 모시고 하나님의 자녀로 살게 됨을 감사합니다.
2. 성령을 부어 주신 하나님께 감사를 드립니다.
3. 나의 영의 눈을 뜨게 해 주신 하나님께 감사합니다.
4. 나의 마음이 항상 주님의 음성을 듣게 하심을 감사합니다.

3. With Thanksgiving

In this world there are those who live with a grateful heart, and those who live complaining all their life. Some live in thatch-roofed huts and are thankful, and others live in mansions and palaces but still feel a sense of void. Some, though they have received little, remember the grace in giving and live with thanksgiving for the grace they've been shown.

All who receive Christ as their Savior are able to live with thanksgiving. And there is no way to contain this thanksgiving that gushes out like a spring each day. Even when I was poor, my heart was daily filled with thanksgiving. My mother was bedridden for six years, yet she never ceased to give thanks. When church members visited her to comfort her, they received greater blessings, seeing my mother's heart of thanksgiving. Every morning, I give thanks to the Lord for giving me peaceful rest overnight and for giving me life to face another new day. Here are just a few reasons why I am grateful to the Lord:

1. I thank God for sending me Jesus Christ to be my Savior and for calling me to be His child.
2. I thank God for anointing me with the Holy Spirit.
3. I thank God for opening the eyes of my heart.
4. I thank God for opening the ears of my heart to hear His voice.

5. 많은 지혜를 주신 하나님께 감사합니다.

6. 예수님을 사랑하는 마음이 일생 동안 변치 않음을 감사
합니다.

7. 지혜로운 어머님께로 어릴 때부터 하나님 진리를 배우
게 됨을 감사합니다.

8. 매일 우물과 같은 기쁨을 넘치게 주신 하나님께 감사합
니다.

9. 아가페의 사랑을 주신 하나님께 감사합니다.

10. 아름다운 음성을 주신 하나님께 감사합니다.

11. 두 눈이 밝아 하나님 지으신 만물을 볼 수 있게 해 주심
을 감사합니다.

12. 성령의 열매 중 가장 귀한 절제의 영을 부어 주심을 하
나님께 감사합니다.

13. 하나님 곡간을 맡은 청지기 됨을 알 수 있는 은혜 주심
을 감사합니다.

14. 한국 여성 되어 아름다운 한복을 입고 전통 예법을 배울
수 있어 감사합니다.

나의 감사한 조건을 다 쓰려면 한이 없어서 이만 줄인다.

5. I thank God for giving me His abundant wisdom.

6. I thank God for giving me an undivided heart of love for Christ.

7. I thank God for giving me a wise mother who taught me about the Truth from my childhood.

8. I thank God for filling me with springs of joy each day.

9. I thank God for His *agape*.

10. I thank God for granting me a beautiful voice.

11. I thank God for giving me two eyes to see the wonderful work of His hand.

12. I thank God for granting me a temperate soul.

13. I thank God for making me a steward of God's storehouse of blessings.

14. I thank God for making me Korean, for allowing me to wear beautiful *hanbok*, and for giving me the opportunity to learn traditional customs.

4. 찬양

　감사하게도 나는 하나님께 찬양의 은사를 받았다. 우리가 우리 마음에 하나님 앞에 가리우는 것이 있으면 입술에서 찬양이 나오지 않는다. 찬양은 멜로디가 붙은 하나님께 드리는 기도의 제사이다. 나는 아침에 일어나서 주방에 들어가면 찬양이 마치 우물과 같이 솟아오른다. 16세 때 편도선 수술을 하고 너무 아파서 하나님께 이런 기도를 드렸다. "하나님 아버지, 저의 목이 나을 때 아름다운 음성을 주시옵소서. 그리하시면 이 음성으로 평생 주님만 찬양하겠습니다." 하나님의 축복으로 나의 음성은 점점 아름다워졌다. 평양신학교에 가서 음악 선생님께 발탁되어 합창단에 들어가 좋은 찬양을 많이 배우고 발표도 했다. 교회 찬양대에 20여 년 독창자로 봉사하는 동안 매일매일 음성이 더 좋아졌다.

　6·25동란이 지나고 아직도 이곳 저곳에서 게릴라전이 있을 때였다. 대구 대봉교회에 24일 밤 크리스마스 축하 예배 시간이 되었다. 항상 나의 독창은 예배 순서 제일 마지막에 있었다. 그날 이상근 목사님이 강대상에 서시더니 "도저히 너무 혼란해서 예배를 느릴 수가 없습니다. 이 집사님, 독창부터 해 주세요." 하셨다. 나는 순종하는 마음으로 강대상에 서니, 교인들이 앉은 자리가 요란해서 마치 파도 치는 것처럼 사람들

4. Praise

My singing talent is a gift from God. When we try to conceal things in our heart from God, songs of praise cannot come from our mouth. Hymns are musical prayers. When I get up early in the morning and go to the kitchen to start the day, songs of praise flow from my mouth like springs of water. When I was sixteen years old, I had my tonsils removed. I felt so much pain that I prayed to God, "Heavenly Father, when my throat heals, please let me have a beautiful voice, and with this voice, I will praise you all my life." I recovered and my voice gradually became more and more beautiful with God's blessing. When I attended Pyeongyang Woman's Theological Seminary, I was selected by my music teacher to be in the choir. I learned many hymns and performed in several public concerts. My voice became more and more beautiful with each of the twenty years I served as a soloist at our church.

Although the Korean War was over, there was still guerrilla warfare going on. The Daebong Presbyterian Church in Daegu was holding its annual Christmas Eve Service. As usual, my solo was to be the last performance, but Reverend Sang Keun Lee stood in front of the altar and said: "There's too much chaos and disorder outside; I cannot start my sermon. Elderwoman Yeu, please sing your solo

이 동요하고 있음을 볼 수 있었다. 상황이 심상치 않았다. 나는 조용히 하나님께 기도드리며 도우심을 구했다. 그리고 나서 나는 성령께서 힘 주시는 대로 '거룩한 밤'을 크고 은혜롭게 불렀다. 온 청중들은 물을 끼얹은 것과 같이 조용해졌다. 이상근 목사님께서 설교를 하시고 우리는 성탄 축하 예배를 은혜롭게 드렸다.

그 다음날 아침에 뉴스를 들으니 대구 제일교회에서 같은 시간에 어떤 사람이 고의적으로 전등 스위치를 끄고 "불이야!" 하고 소리를 질렀다고 한다. 서로들 먼저 나가려고 하다가 어린 생명들이 여러 명 밟혀서 죽고 수 많은 사람이 다치는 불상사가 있었음을 알게 되었다. 6·25 후에 남한에 남아 있던 좌익들의 책동이었다. 하나님께서 같은 날 밤 부족한 나의 찬양을 들어 쓰셔서 큰 불행에서 우리 교회를 지켜주신 것에 대해 나는 감사를 드렸다. 이와 함께 찬양의 힘이 이렇게 큰 효과가 있는 줄 다시 한번 깨닫게 되었다. 찬송은 우리 믿는 자에게 주시는 가장 큰 하나님의 은사이다.

first." I stood up with a submissive heart and was able to see that the church members felt no peace within. They were restless, moving about like waves in the sea. I quietly prayed to God for His help, and with the presence of the Holy Spirit in me, I sang "Oh, Holy Night" as gracefully as I could with a loud voice. The congregation became silent like a calm sea. Reverend Sang Keun Lee then proceeded to preach his sermon, and we concluded the Christmas worship service with God's grace.

The next day, I heard on the news about a tragedy that occurred the previous night at Jeil Presbyterian Church in Daegu. One man intentionally pulled the fire alarm and yelled "Fire!" The congregation panicked, and trying to get out quickly, they trampled on a number of children, killing them, and left many more injured. This tragic event was planned by North Korean guerillas that had remained in hiding in the South after the end of the Korean War. I was extremely grateful that God kept our church safe in the midst of chaos and that He had used my voice to restore peace in the lives of those He loved. I experienced the great power of our praises to the Lord. I believe the call to praise God is the greatest gift we who believe have been granted.

5. 안식일

　안식일은 하나님께서 우리 인생들에게 복 주시려고 약속하신 날이다. 나는 어릴 때 어머님으로부터 이런 교육을 받았다. 교회에 가려고 저고리를 입다가 옷고름이 떨어지면 어머님은 바느질을 허락하지 않으셨다. 그리고 "애야, 네 저고리가 하나밖에 없니? 거룩한 안식일에는 예배에만 집중하도록 하여라."고 말씀하셨다. 내가 자랄 때 주일이 되면 오전에 성경 공부와 예배를 드리고 오후에는 유년 주일학교를 가르치고 찬양을 연습하고 저녁 식사 후에는 밤 예배를 참석했다. 우리는 하루 종일 기름진 주님의 동산에서 은혜의 양식을 먹게 된다. 주일날 이렇게 기쁘게 지내면 다음 한 주간 생활은 즐거움과 기쁨의 연속일 수 밖에 없다.

　하나님께서 안식하신 날, 우리 인간이 범하면 어찌하겠나! 대구 대봉교회에 가려면 언제나 냇물가를 지나간다. 주일이면 아낙네들이 빨래를 많이 한다. 나는 그곳을 지날 때마다 "하나님 아버지, 감사합니다. 나도 예수님을 모르고 살았으면 저런 사람들과 같이 항상 분주한 생활을 했을 터인데, 일찍 주님을 믿고 일주일에 하루를 쉴 수 있는 축복을 주신 하나님께 감사를 드립니다."하며 늘 기도드렸다.

5. Sabbath

The Sabbath is a day of rest on which God promises to give His people blessings. My mother taught me from childhood that the Sabbath was such a day. Even if my coat strap were to come loose, my mother would not permit any sewing on the Sabbath. She would say, "My dear, do you have just one coat? Focus only on Sunday service on the Lord's holy day." Growing up, I attended Sunday service and Bible study class in the morning, taught Sunday school and practiced with the church choir in the afternoon, and attended the evening service afterwards. From dawn to dusk every Sunday, our family received God's anointing and spiritual food in His fruitful garden. A joyful Sunday would prepare my heart to expect the greater joys I was bound to experience in the days to come.

God rested on the Sabbath. Who then would dare not to rest? On my way to Daebong Presbyterian Church on Sundays, I would walk past a group of women washing clothes by the stream. Every time I passed by, I prayed, "Heavenly Father, thank You. If I had not come to know Christ, I too, like these women, would be living a busy life, stripped of rest. Thank You for giving me faith in You and for giving me rest in You."

6. 거룩함

나는 어린 시절 이 말씀에 큰 은혜를 받았다. 우리 아버지가 대통령이면 우리는 행동을 아주 조심해야 한다. 하물며 이 우주의 권세를 주관하시는 하나님의 자녀 된 우리들이 거룩함에 속하여야 한다. 나는 아이들에게 항상 이런 말을 했다. "우리가 이 세상에서 바른 말도 다 못하고 사는데 어찌 옳지 않은 말을 할 수 있겠니 그러니 항상 덕스러운 말만 하고 살자. 그리고 거짓말은 절대로 하지 말자. 거짓말을 하는 자는 하나님의 나라에 들어갈 권리가 없다." 나의 어머님은 항상 행동이 거룩하셨고, 모든 일에 침착하셔서 교인들의 존경과 신뢰를 받으셨다. 당회에서 도저히 해결할 수 없는 일이 있으면 어머님께 도움을 요청하셨다. 하나님은 거룩하신 분이시다. 믿음으로 하나님의 자녀가 되었으니 우리는 마땅히 거룩하게 살아야 할 것이다.

6. Holiness

[16]Be holy, because I am holy.
(1 Peter 1:16)

I received abundant grace in my childhood from this passage. If your father is the president, you are expected to be cautious in your conduct. Then, as children of the Father of all creation, we must live in His holiness. I always told my children: "An entire lifetime is still not long enough to say all the wonderful things we have to say. How then could we waste time saying what is rash? Let us have only edifying words on our lips. Let us never lie, for the kingdom of God has no place for a liar." My mother's every move was made in God's holiness. She was always calm and gained much respect from the members of the congregation. Any time the elders at church faced a difficult situation, they would ask my mother for advice. God is holy. We must lead holy lives to be worthy of His calling as His children.

7. 십일조에 대하여

　　내가 어릴 때 부모님께서 항상 십일조를 드렸다. 나도 출가해서 십일조를 드렸다. 이것은 하나님을 섬기는 자의 마땅한 예법이다. 우리는 모두 빈손 들고 와서 빈손 들고 가는 인생을 살고 있다. 세상에서 우리는 하나님의 곡간을 맡은 청지기에 지나지 않는다. 이러한 신념으로 살면 물욕이 없어지고 항상 겸손할 수 있다. 자기 것이 아닌 물질로 교만할 수 없다. 십일조를 철저히 드릴수록 큰 축복을 받는다. 하늘 문을 여시고 내리신 하나님의 축복이다. 나는 내 모든 것이 하나님께서 주신 축복임을 분명히 증거한다.

7. Tithing

My parents always tithed (an offering of a tenth of one's income to God. *Editor's note*) since I could remember. I began to tithe when I married. This is required of all who serve God. We are born without possessions, and we die without possessions. We are stewards of God's household. If we live with this in mind, we can protect ourselves from greed and material attachment, and live a humble life, free from foolish pride over what we do not own. The more faithfully you tithe, the greater the blessings you are sure to receive. God will open the gates of heaven and send you showers of blessings. I will surely testify that all that I have has come from the Lord.

8. 이적

현재 20세기에 사는 대부분의 사람들은 이적을 부인한다. 과학 문명이 발달되어 달나라까지 가는 이 마당에 이적이 무엇이냐고 한다. 반면에 그들의 일상 속에서 매일 기적을 경험하는 사람들도 있다. 내가 소녀 때 일이다. 그때 우리나라에는 김익두 목사님이 계셨다. 이분은 젊었을 때 어찌나 못된 불량배였던지 시장에 가는 상인들이 "오늘 시장에 갔다가 올 때 김익두 안 만나게 해 주세요."하고 빌었다고 한다. 그렇게 악랄하던 사람이 예수님을 믿고 회개하여 딴 사람이 되었다. 그는 신학을 해서 목사가 되고 성령의 충만함을 받고 많은 병자들을 고쳤다. 그러던 중 내가 중학교 일학년 때 나의 선배 언니가 시력을 잃었는데, 그때 마침 우리 남산교회에 부흥회 강사님으로 김익두 목사님께서 오셨다. 나는 그 선배 언니가 김익두 목사님의 안수기도를 받고 눈이 나아서 공부를 계속하여 졸업하는 것을 보았다. 그때 어찌나 크게 감격했던지!

우리 하나님은 지금도 많은 기도의 종들을 통하여 역사하신다. 대구 절제회 박귀순 권사님은 1964년 자궁암에 걸려서 수술을 시작했는데, 암이 너무 깊이 진행되어 수술 불능이었다. 그러나 어떤 권사님의 기도를 받고 완쾌되어 그 후 교회를 세 곳에 건립했다. 이 지구상에 오늘도 하나님의 이적은 무한

8. Miracles

People in the twentieth century often live with the belief that miracles, in this era of science where even trips to the moon are possible, do not happen. Still, there are those who experience miracles in their daily lives. In our country there lived a terrible delinquent named Ik Doo Kim. Whenever his townspeople went to the market, they said, "I hope I don't run into him on my way to and from the market." This vicious man met Christ one day and repented, and he became a whole new person. He went to seminary and became a pastor. He was filled with the Holy Spirit and God gave him the spiritual gift of healing. I myself saw something miraculous happen through him in my first year of middle school. One of the older students at school had a sister who had gone blind. Pastor Ik Doo Kim was invited to lead a revival service at Namsan Presbyterian Church one day. When he laid his hands on her and prayed for her, she was immediately healed. She was able to continue her studies and she later graduated. This miraculous event deeply moved my heart and has left a great impact on my life!

Even today, God is working His miracles through His servants' faithful prayers. In 1964, Daegu KWCTU member Deaconess Kwi Soon Park was diagnosed with uterine cancer and had to undergo surgery. The cancer, unfortunately, had already spread, so the doctors weren't able to remove the tumors. Miraculously, Deaconess Kwi Soon Park was

히 계속되고 있다. 나는 내 나름대로 체험한 이적을 몇 가지 적어 보려고 한다.

1. 술 마시던 나의 아버지가 예수님을 믿고 술을 끊고 어질고 착하게 일생을 사시다가 마지막 자기가 가시는 시간을 정확하게 아신 것은 이적이었다.
2. 기역, 니은도 안 배우신 어머님이 예수님을 믿고 성령의 충만함을 받아 성경 선생님이 되셔서 거룩한 일생을 보내신 것은 이적이었다.
3. 내가 절제회관을 구입할 때 가장 어려운 시절에 미국에서 5,000불의 돈이 온 것은 큰 이적이었다.
4. 나는 인격만 보고 물질도 빈곤하고 믿음도 빈곤한 가정으로 시집을 왔는데, 지금 물질도 차고 넘치며 친척들이 다 예수님을 믿는 놀라운 이적을 체험했다.

우리는 한센병자가 낫고 벙어리가 말하는 것만 이적인 줄 안다. 그러나 죄에 빠진 사람이 회개하고 예수님을 믿어 의인이 되는 이적이 더욱 큰 이적이다.

completely healed through the power of prayer. She helped establish three churches. God works miracles everywhere on earth. Here are just a few miracles I have witnessed:

1. My father quit drinking alcohol after he received Christ as his Savior and lived with a merciful and benevolent heart. He knew, in the last moments of his life, the exact time that he would go to be with God.
2. My mother, who had never learned to read, became a Bible study leader after she accepted Christ into her life. She lived a holy life, filled with the Holy Spirit.
3. When we were looking for funding for the KWCTU Hall, we received $5,000 from the U.S. to pay for the purchase of the hall.
4. I married into a family that lacked both money and faith, but now we have gained wealth and all my in-laws have become Christians.

When we think of miracles, we often think about lepers and deaf-mutes being healed, but it is an even greater miracle when a sinner repents and comes to know Christ, and when a sinner is regarded as righteous before God through faith in Jesus.

9. 태교

　　나는 어머님으로부터 태교에 대하여 배웠다. 옷을 만드는 과정에 비교하면, 아이가 어머니 뱃속에 있을 때 받는 교육은 옷감을 짜는 것과 같은 것이요, 가정교육은 재단을 하는 것과 같고, 학교교육은 바느질에 지나지 않는다고 하셨다. 나는 아이를 가지면 성경 외에 모든 독서를 중지했다. 남편은 내게 물었다. "그러면 세상 소식에 너무 차단이 되지 않소." 나는 대답했다. "기쁜 뉴스만 전해주세요." 먼데서 싸움하는 소리가 나면 나는 귀를 씻었다. 나는 항상 하나님께 찬양과 감사를 드렸다. 하나님께서 주신 귀한 자녀는 한 생명 한 생명이 모두 아름다운 특징을 가지고 있다. 나는 지금도 감사한다. 이 태교에 대하여 가르쳐주신 어머님과 이렇게 잘 길러 주신 하나님께 매일 감사를 드린다.

　　우리 여성들의 인격은 나 한 사람의 것이 아니다. 자녀와 남편에게 얼마나 큰 영향을 주는지 우리는 분명하게 알아야 된다. 나는 어머님이 나를 가지시고 태교 하신 이야기를 들을 때마다 행복하고 감사했다. 더욱이 아이를 낳는 여자들이 술을 마신다는 것은 매우 두려운 일이다. 앞으로 원자탄보다 더 무서운 일이 술을 마시고 낳는 자녀들이다. 이 사회에는 많은 범죄들이 있다. 이 모든 범죄가 은밀히 따지면 술을 마시고

9. Prenatal Education

My mother taught me about the importance of prenatal education. The development of a child can be likened to the making of clothes. Prenatal education is the stage where a piece of cloth or fabric is woven; family education is when the measuring and cutting of fabric into different shapes and sizes occurs; and school education is when the pieces of fabric are sewn together to create a unique whole. When I became pregnant, I stopped reading all books, other than the Bible. My husband asked me one day, "Don't you feel like you're isolating yourself from everything that is occurring around you?" I replied, "Please only share with me good news." When I heard someone fighting in the background, I covered my ears. I always praised God and thanked Him. Each child is a precious gift from God and each is born with a beautiful, unique personality. I remain grateful for my children. I'm grateful for my mother's lessons on prenatal care, and my heart of thanksgiving is renewed daily for God's nurturing of my children with His grace.

So many times we forget how much we really do affect others. A woman needs to recognize how great an impact she has on her husband and children. Whenever I heard about how my mother valued prenatal education and was careful when I was still in her womb, I was filled with great joy and

낳은 부모들의 죄악의 씨들이다. 우리가 인류 사회에서 술을
몰아 내어야만 이 사회가 깨끗해질 것이다.

gratitude. Alcohol is extremely dangerous to the developing fetus. The outcomes, both direct and indirect, are at times more horrifying than a detonated atomic bomb. Society is already full of crime. Many crime cases trace back to poor parenting and alcohol. We must strive to expel alcohol from our society in order to clean up our society.

10. 기도

　우리는 세상을 살 때 여러 가지 일들에 부딪힌다. 우리는 이럴 때 항상 기도해야 한다. 나는 아침에 일어나면 먼저 하나님의 말씀을 봉독하고 하나님께 기도를 드렸다. 이것은 하나님께 먼저 인사를 드리는 것과 같다. 그리고 하루 종일 일을 하면 모든 일이 순조롭게 된다. 우리의 기도는 신앙생활에 있어서 호흡과 같은 것이다. 아무리 건강한 사람이라도 5분만 숨을 쉬지 않으면 생명을 유지할 수 없듯이 우리가 참된 그리스도인이 되려면 늘 기도에 힘써야 한다.

　성경 말씀에 "항상 기뻐하라, 쉬지 말고 기도하라, 범사에 감사하라."(데살로니가전서 5:16~18)고 하셨다. 우리가 쉬지 않고 기도하는 것은 정말 기쁜 생활이다. 모든 만사를 하나님께 기도드림으로 맡기고 하나님의 동산의 귀한 자녀로서 항상 기도하는 생활을 하면 우리의 삶은 하나님의 인도하심으로 더욱 아름다워진다.

　내가 처음 시집왔을 때 다른 친척들은 다 부자로 살고 있었는데, 그때 나의 시댁은 참 가난했다. 그러나 나는 부자 친척들을 한번도 무러워하시 않고 오이러 불쌍히 여겼다. 나는 그들을 위해서 늘 축복기도를 해주었다. 그 많은 축복기도가 응답되어, 수십 년 세월이 흐르는 동안 하나님께서 그 분들의 영

10. Prayer

We experience all forms of trials and tribulations while living in this world. We need to develop the discipline of prayer from childhood. Every morning, I meditate upon God's Word and pray. It's my way of saying "Good morning" to God first thing in the morning. You'll be surprised to see how much the quality of your daily life changes when you start your day with prayer and meditation upon God's living Word. Each prayer is like a breath to the spiritual life. Just as we cannot go without breathing, our spiritual life must breathe the breath of prayer without ceasing. For it is written:

[16]Be joyful always; [17]pray continually;
[18]give thanks in all circumstances,
for this is God's will for you in Christ Jesus.
(1 Thessalonians 5:16-18)

A life led in prayer is a truly joyous life. When we lay down all our cares at His feet through prayer, and when we pray without ceasing as children of God, our lives shine more beautifully because of His guidance.

During the early years of my marriage to Soo Keun, all our relatives but my husband' s family were rich. But I had compassion toward them, for though they were with material wealth, they were without Christ. God planted in my heart the desire to pray for them. And He answered my prayers for

혼을 모두 구원해주셨다.

기 도

기도는 인생 길을 밝히는 등불이요

기도는 주의 영광 보이는 시간이요

기도는 주님 품 안에 안기우는 순간이요

기도는 괴로움을 없애는 순간이요

기도는 우리들의 소원을 이루시는 시간이요

기도는 주의 축복 내리시는 시간이요

(1971년 8월)

their salvation several decades later. God saved each and
every one of them.

Prayer

(August 1971)

Prayer is the lamp that illuminates the path of life.

Prayer is a time when God's glory is revealed.

Prayer is a moment for throwing yourself into His arms.

Prayer is a moment for removing all afflictions.

Prayer is a time for Him to fulfill our hopes.

Prayer is a time for receiving His blessings.

Chapter 5

The Word of God Which Leads My Life

나를 인도하신 하나님의 말씀

하바드에서 신학석사
학위 받은 셋째 아들 김영훈
Younghoon received his Master of
Divinity degree from Harvard (1989)

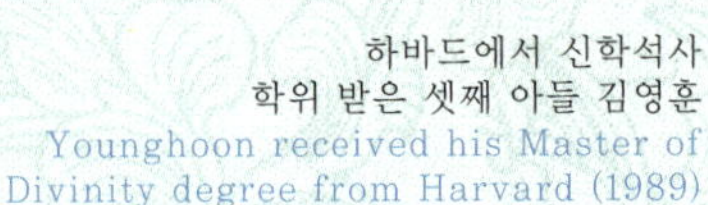

원일한 박사와 RAS (왕립아시아학회) 활동
The Daesung Group Chairman Younghoon David Kim and
Dr. Horace G. Underwood of the Royal Asiatic Society

1970년 영락교회 한경직 목사님과 영락모자원 성탄 축하 예배
Christmas service at the Youngnak Shelter for Widows and their Children with Reverend Kyung Jik Han of Youngnak Presbyterian Church (1970)

1990년 영락여자신학원 후원회 회장 시절
Days as chairwoman of the supporting committee for the Youngnak Woman's Theological Seminary (1990)

영락교회 권사로 20년 근속기념 수상
Receiving the 20 Year Service Award as elderwoman at Youngnak Presbyterian Church (1989)

1. 내 가정과 내 자녀들을 이끌어 복 받게 하신 하나님의 말씀

나는 체험하였다. 예수님께서 주시는 기쁨과 평안을! 초가집에서 시집살이 시절, 손에 피가 날 때도 나는 항상 기쁨이 넘쳐 흘렀다. 중한 병상에서도 내게 이 기쁨이 흘러 넘쳤다. 이렇게 일생을 살다 보니 나의 생은 기쁨의 생이었다. 아이들도 다 이 기쁨을 체험하고 있다. 하나같이 다 친구들에게 친절하며 항상 방실방실 웃고 있다. 이 기쁨은 예수님을 믿지 않는 자는 알지 못하는 기쁨이다.

솟아나는 기쁨과 평안은 하나님의 선물이다.우리가 우리의 죄를 자복하고 하나님을 나의 아버지로 부르고 예수님을 나의 구주로 모시면, 이 평화와 기쁨의 복을 받게 된다. 부자나 가난한 자나 옥에 갇힌 자나 누구든지 주님 앞에 나와서 겸손히 무릎을 꿇으면, 주님은 아가페의 사랑으로 당신을 용서해 주시고 그 거룩하시고 참되신 기쁨과 평화를 선물로 주실 줄 믿는다.

나는 내 평생에 나를 인도하신 하나님의 말씀 중에서 주시는 은혜에 따라 특히 다음 말씀을 기록하고 싶다. 내 평생토록 나를 인도하시고 내 가정과 내 자녀들을 이끌어 복 받게 하신 하나님 이 말씀을 읽고 아직두 믿지 않는 분들이 있으면, 모두 예수님 앞에 나와 불신의 죄를 자복하고 예수 그리스도를 믿음으로 함께 영생을 받게 되시기를 간절히 바란다.

1. The Source of Blessings for My Life and Family

I have experienced God's unspeakable joy and peace! I felt overflowing joy even when my hands bled from doing all the household chores. Even when I was seriously ill, I was filled with the fullness of His joy. And because I lived with a joyful heart, my life was full of joy. My children too have come to experience God's joy. They are always kind to their friends and always have a cheerful look on their faces. This joy is known only to those who believe in Christ.

Overflowing peace and joy are just two of God's many gifts. If we confess our sins, call God our Father, and accept Christ as our Savior, we will receive His blessings of peace and joy. If the rich and the poor, the healthy and sick, and the imprisoned alike kneel down before the Lord, then, with His *agape* love, God will forgive them and give them the complete and holy gift of peace and joy.

I would like to make special note of several Scripture verses that God has blessed me through and has used to guide me throughout all the days of my life. These words have blessed not only me but also my family and children by bringing to us His grace. I pray that all who, even after reading the following Scripture verses, still do not believe may soon accept Christ, confess their sins, become free with a faith in Christ, and receive God's gracious gift of eternal life.

시편 4:7 - 8

주께서 내 마음에 두신 기쁨은

그들의 곡식과 새 포도주의 풍성할 때보다 더하니이다.

내가 평안히 눕고 자기도 하리니

나를 안전히 살게 하시는 이는 오직 여호와시니이다.

빌립보서 4:4

주 안에서 항상 기뻐하라,

내가 다시 말하노니 기뻐하라.

빌립보서 2:4

각각 자기 일을 돌볼뿐더러, 또한 각각

다른 사람들의 일을 돌보아 나의 기쁨을 충만하게 하라.

마태복음 5:11 - 12

나로 말미암아 너희를 욕하고 박해하고

거짓으로 너희를 거슬러 모든 악한 말을 할 때에는

너희에게 복이 있나니

기뻐하고 즐거워하라, 하늘에서 너희의 상이 큼이라.

너희 전에 있던 선지자들도 이같이 박해하였느니라.

2. Scriptures on Joy

(Psalm 4:7-8)

[7]You have filled my heart with greater joy than when their grain and new wine abound. [8]I will lie down and sleep in peace, for you alone, O LORD, make me dwell in safety.

(Philippians 4:4)

[4]Rejoice in the LORD always.
I will say it again: Rejoice!

(Philippians 2:4)

[4]Each of you should look not only to your own interests, but also to the interests of others.

(Matthew 5:11-12)

[11] Blessed are you when people insult you, persecute you and falsely say all kinds of evil against you because of me. [12]Rejoice and be glad, because great is your reward in heaven, for in the same way they persecuted the prophets who were before you.

시편 16:11

주께서 생명의 길을 내게 보이시리니,

주의 앞에는 충만한 기쁨이 있고

주의 오른쪽에는 영원한 즐거움이 있나이다.

시편 19:7 - 10

여호와의 율법은 완전하여 영혼을 소성시키시며,

여호와의 증거는 확실하여 우둔한 자를 지혜롭게 하며,

여호와의 교훈은 정직하여 마음을 기쁘게 하고,

여호와의 계명은 순결하여 눈을 밝게 하시도다.

여호와를 경외하는 도는 정결하여 영원까지 이르고,

여호와의 법도 진실하여 다 의로우니,

금 곧 많은 순금보다 더 사모할 것이며

꿀과 송이꿀보다 더 달도다.

시편 21:1

여호와여 왕이 주의 힘으로 말미암아 기뻐하며

주의 구원으로 말미암아 크게 즐거워하리이다.

(Psalm 16:11)

¹¹*You have made known to me the path of life;*

you will fill me with joy in your presence,

with eternal pleasures at your right hand.

(Psalm 19:7-10)

⁷*The law of the LORD is perfect, reviving the soul.*

The statutes of the LORD are trustworthy, making wise the simple.

⁸*The precepts of the LORD are right, giving joy to the heart.*

The commands of the LORD are radiant, giving light to the eyes.

⁹*The fear of the LORD is pure, enduring forever.*

The ordinances of the LORD are sure and altogether righteous.

¹⁰*They are more precious than gold, than much pure gold;*

they are sweeter than honey, than honey from the comb.

(Psalm 21:1)

¹*O LORD, the king rejoices in your strength.*

How great is his joy in the victories you give!

시편 28:7

여호와는 나의 힘과 나의 방패이시니
내 마음이 그를 의지하여 도움을 얻었도다.
그러므로 내 마음이 크게 기뻐하며
내 노래로 그를 찬송하리로다.

시편 30:11

주께서 나의 슬픔이 변하여 내게 춤이 되게 하시며,
나의 베옷을 벗기고 기쁨으로 띠 띠우셨나이다.

시편 97:11

의인을 위하여 빛을 뿌리고
마음이 정직한 자를 위하여 기쁨을 뿌리시는도다.

시편 100:1 - 2

온 땅은 여호와께 즐거운 찬송을 부를지어다.
기쁨으로 여호와를 섬기며
노래하면서 그의 앞에 나아갈지어다.

(Psalm 28:7)

[7]The LORD is my strength and my shield;

my heart trusts in him, and I am helped.

My heart leaps for joy

and I will give thanks to him in song.

(Psalm 30:11)

[11]You turned my wailing into dancing; you removed my

sackcloth and clothed me with joy.

(Psalm 97:11)

[11]Light is shed upon the righteous

and joy on the upright in heart.

(Psalm 100:1-2)

[1]Shout for joy to the LORD, all the earth.

[2]Worship the LORD with gladness;

come before him with joyful songs.

3. 평화에 대한 성구

누가복음 2:14

지극히 높은 곳에서는 하나님께 영광이요,

땅에서는 하나님이 기뻐하신 사람들 중에 평화로다.

이사야 26:3

주께서 심지가 견고한 자를 평강하고 평강하도록 지키시리니,

이는 그가 주를 신뢰함이니이다.

이사야 26:12

여호와여 주께서 우리를 위하여 평강을 베푸시오리니,

주께서 우리의 모든 일도 우리를 위하여 이루심이니이다.

이사야 53:5 - 6

그가 찔림은 우리의 허물 때문이요,

그가 상함은 우리의 죄악 때문이라.

그가 징계를 받음으로 우리는 평화를 누리고,

그가 채찍에 맞으므로 우리가 나음을 받았도다.

우리는 다 양 같아서 그릇 행하여 각기 제 길로 갔거늘,

여호와께서는 우리 모두의 죄악을 그에게 담당시키셨도다.

3. Scriptures on Peace

(Luke 2:14)

[14] *"Glory to God in the highest,*

and on earth peace to men on whom his favor rests."

(Isaiah 26:3)

[3] *You will keep in perfect peace him whose mind is steadfast,*

because he trusts in you.

(Isaiah 26:12)

[12] *LORD, you establish peace for us;*

all that we have accomplished you have done for us.

(Isaiah 53:5-6)

[5] *But he was pierced for our transgressions, he was crushed*

for our iniquities; the punishment that brought us peace was

upon him, and by his wounds we are healed.

[6] *We all, like sheep, have gone astray, each of us has turned to*

his own way; and the LORD has laid on him

the iniquity of us all.

시편 37:37

온전한 사람을 살피고 정직한 자를 볼지어다.
모든 화평한 자의 미래는 평안이로다.

시편 119:165

주의 법을 사랑하는 자에게는 큰 평안이 있으니
그들에게 장애물이 없으리이다.

요한복음 14:27

평안을 너희에게 끼치노니 곧 나의 평안을 너희에게 주노라.
내가 너희에게 주는 것은 세상이 주는 것과 같지 아니하니라.
너희는 마음에 근심하지도 말고 두려워하지도 말라.

요한복음 16:33

이것을 너희에게 이르는 것은
너희로 내 안에서 평안을 누리게 하려 함이라.
세상에서는 너희가 환난을 당하나 담대하라.
내가 세상을 이기었노라.

(Psalm 37:37)

[37]*Consider the blameless, observe the upright;*

there is a future for the man of peace.

(Psalm 119:165)

[165]*Great peace have they who love your law,*

and nothing can make them stumble.

(John 14:27)

[27] *"Peace I leave with you; my peace I give you.*

I do not give to you as the world gives.

Do not let your hearts be troubled and do not be afraid."

(John 16:33)

[33] *"I have told you these things,*

so that in me you may have peace.

In this world you will have trouble.

But take heart! I have overcome the world."

4. 믿음에 대한 성구

요한복음 1:12

영접하는 자 곧 그 이름을 믿는 자들에게는
하나님의 자녀가 되는 권세를 주셨으니.

요한복음 3:16

하나님이 세상을 이처럼 사랑하사 독생자를 주셨으니,
이는 그를 믿는 자마다 멸망하지 않고
영생을 얻게 하려 하심이니라.

요한복음 3:36

아들을 믿는 자에게는 영생이 있고
아들을 순종하지 아니하는 자는 영생을 보지 못하고
도리어 하나님의 진노가 그 위에 머물러 있느니라.

요한복음 4:41 – 42

예수의 말씀으로 말미암아 믿는 자가 더욱 많아
그 여자에게 말하되, 이제 우리가 믿는 것은
네 말로 인함이 아니니 이는 우리가 친히 듣고
그가 참으로 세상의 구주신 줄 앎이라 하였더라.

4. Scriptures on Faith

(John 1:12)

[12] *Yet to all who received Him, to those who believed in his*

name, he gave the right to become children of God.

(John 3:16)

[16] *"For God so loved the world that he gave his one and only*

Son, that whoever believes in him shall not perish

but have eternal life."

(John 3:36)

[36] *Whoever believes in the Son has eternal life,*

but whoever rejects the Son will not see life,

for God's wrath remains on him.

(John 4:41-42)

[41] *And because of his words many more became believers.*

[42] *They said to the woman, "We no longer believe just*

because of what you said; now we have heard for ourselves,

and we know that

this man really is the Savior of the world."

요한복음 5:24

내가 진실로 진실로 너희에게 이르노니

내 말을 듣고 또 나 보내신 이를 믿는 자는

영생을 얻었고 심판에 이르지 아니하나니

사망에서 생명으로 옮겼느니라.

요한복음 6:29

하나님께서 보내신 이를 믿는 것이 하나님의 일이니라.

요한복음 6:35

예수께서 이르시되 나는 생명의 떡이니

내게 오는 자는 결코 주리지 아니할 터이요,

나를 믿는 자는 영원히 목마르지 아니하리라.

요한복음 6:40

내 아버지의 뜻은 아들을 보고 믿는 자마다

영생을 얻는 이것이니,

마지막 날에 내가 이를 다시 살리리라 하시니라.

요한복음 6:47 - 48

진실로 진실로 너희에게 이르노니,

믿는 자는 영생을 가졌나니 내가 곧 생명의 떡이니라.

(John 5:24)

²⁴ *"I tell you the truth,*

whoever hears my word and believes him

who sent me has eternal life and will not be condemned;

he has crossed over from death to life."

(John 6:29)

²⁹*Jesus answered, "The work of God is this:*

to believe in the one he has sent."

(John 6:35)

³⁵*Then Jesus declared, "I am the bread of life.*

He who comes to me will never go hungry,

and he who believes in me will never be thirsty."

(John 6:40)

⁴⁰ *"For my Father's will is that everyone who looks to the Son*

and believes in him shall have eternal life, and I will raise

him up at the last day."

(John 6:47-48)

⁴⁷ *"I tell you the truth, he who believes has*

everlasting life. ⁴⁸I am the bread of life."

요한복음 7:38 - 39

나를 믿는 자는 성경에 이름과 같이

그 배에서 생수의 강이 흘러 나오리라 하시니,

이는 그를 믿는 자들이 받을 성령을 가리켜 말씀하신 것이라.

요한복음 11:40 - 41

네가 믿으면 하나님의 영광을 보리라 하지 아니하였느냐 하시니,

돌을 옮겨 놓으니 예수께서 눈을 들어 우러러 보시고 이르시되,

아버지여 내 말을 들으신 것을 감사하나이다.

요한복음 12:36

너희에게 아직 빛이 있을 동안에 빛을 믿으라.

그리하면 빛의 아들이 되리라.

요한복음 12:44 - 46

예수께서 외쳐 이르시되 나를 믿는 자는 나를 믿는 것이 아니오

나를 보내신 이를 믿는 것이며, 나를 보는 자는 나를 보내신 이를

보는 것이니라. 나는 빛으로 세상에 왔나니

무릇 나를 믿는 자로 어둠에 거하지 않게 하려 함이로라.

(John 7:38-39)

[38] *"Whoever believes in me, as the Scripture has said,*
streams of living water will flow from within him."
[39] *By this he meant the Spirit, whom those who believed in him*
were later to receive. Up to that time the Spirit had not been
given, since Jesus had not yet been glorified.

(John 11:40-41)

[40] *Then Jesus said, "Did I not tell you that if you believed, you*
would see the glory of God?" [41] So they took away the stone.
Then Jesus looked up and said,
"Father, I thank you that you have heard me."

(John 12:36)

[36] *"Put your trust in the light while you have it,*
so that you may become sons of light."

(John 12:44-46)

[44] *Then Jesus cried out, "When a man believes in me, he does*
not believe in me only, but in the one who sent me.
[45] *When he looks at me, he sees the one who sent me.*
[46] *I have come into the world as a light, so that no one*
who believes in me should stay in darkness."

요한복음 14:1

너희는 마음에 근심하지 말라.

하나님을 믿으니 또 나를 믿으라.

요한복음 14:11 - 12

내가 아버지 안에 거하고 아버지께서 내 안에 계심을 믿으라.

그렇지 못하겠거든 행하는 그 일로 말미암아 나를 믿으라.

내가 진실로 진실로 너희에게 이르노니

나를 믿는 자는 내가 하는 일을 그도 할 것이요,

또한 그보다 큰 일도 하리니 이는 내가 아버지께로 감이라.

요한복음 20:29

예수께서 이르시되 너는 나를 본 고로 믿느냐,

보지 못하고 믿는 자들은 복되도다 하시니라.

요한복음 20:31

오직 이것을 기록함은 너희로 예수께서

하나님의 아들 그리스도이심을 믿게 하려 함이요,

또 너희로 믿고 그 이름을 힘입어 생명을 얻게 하려 함이니라.

(John 14:1)

¹ *"Do not let your hearts be troubled.*

Trust in God; trust also in me."

(John 14:11-12)

¹¹ *"Believe me when I say that I am in the Father and the*

Father is in me; or at least believe on the evidence of the

miracles themselves. ¹²I tell you the truth, anyone who has

faith in me will do what I have been doing. He will do even

greater things than these, because I am going to the Father."

(John 20:29)

²⁹*Then Jesus told him, "Because you have seen me, you have*

believed; blessed are those who have not seen

and yet have believed."

(John 20:31)

³¹*But these are written that you may believe that*

Jesus is the Christ, the Son of God, and that by believing you

may have life in his name.

5. 부활에 대한 성구

요한복음 5:28 - 29

이를 기이히 여기지 말라 무덤 속에 있는 자가

다 그의 음성을 들을 때가 오나니, 선한 일을 행한 자는

생명의 부활로 악한 일을 행한 자는 심판의 부활로 나오리라.

요한복음 6:54

내 살을 먹고 내 피를 마시는 자는 영생을 가졌고

마지막 날에 내가 그를 다시 살리리니.

요한복음 11:25 - 27

예수께서 이르시되 나는 부활이요 생명이니

나를 믿는 자는 죽어도 살겠고

무릇 살아서 나를 믿는 자는 영원히 죽지 아니 하리니

이것을 네가 믿느냐

이르되 주여 그러하외다 주는 그리스도시요

세상에 오시는 하나님의 아들이신 줄 내가 믿나이다.

요한복음 20:15 - 18

예수께서 이르시되 여자여 어찌하여 울며

누구를 찾느냐 하시니

5. Scriptures on Resurrection

(John 5:28-29)

[28] *"Do not be amazed at this, for a time is coming when all who are in their graves will hear his voice* [29]*and come out—those who have done good will rise to live, and those who have done evil will rise to be condemned."*

(John 6:54)

[54] *"Whoever eats my flesh and drinks my blood has eternal life, and I will raise him up at the last day."*

(John 11:25-27)

[25]*Jesus said to her, "I am the resurrection and the life. He who believes in me will live, even though he dies;* [26]*and whoever lives and believes in me will never die. Do you believe this?"* [27] *"Yes, Lord," she told him, "I believe that you are the Christ, the Son of God, who was to come into the world."*

(John 20:15-18)

[15] *"Woman," he said, "why are you crying? Who is it you are looking for?" Thinking he was the gardener,*

마리아는 그가 동산지기인 줄 알고 이르되

주여 당신이 옮겼거든 어디 두었는지 내게 이르소서

그리하면 내가 가져 가리이다 예수께서 마리아야 하시거늘

마리아가 돌이켜 히브리말로 랍오니 하니(이는 선생님이라는 말이라)

예수께서 이르시되 나를 붙들지 말라

내가 아직 아버지께로 올라가지 아니하였노라

너는 내 형제들에게 가서 이르되 내가 내 아버지 곧 너희 아버지

내 하나님 곧 너희 하나님께로 올라간다 하라 하시니

막달라 마리아가 가서 제자들에게 내가 주를 보았다 하고

또 주께서 자기에게 이렇게 말씀하셨다 이르니라.

요한복음 20:21 - 23

예수께서 또 이르시되 너희에게 평강이 있을지어다

아버지께서 나를 보내신 것같이 나도 너희를 보내노라

이 말씀을 하시고 저희를 향하사 숨을 내쉬며 이르시되

성령을 받으라 너희가 누구의 죄든지 사하면 사하여 질 것이요

누구의 죄든지 그대로 두면 그대로 있으리라 하시니라.

요한복음 20:27 - 28

도마에게 이르시되 네 손가락을 이리 내밀어

내 손을 보고 네 손을 내밀어 내 옆구리에 넣어보라

she said, "Sir, if you have carried him away, tell me where

you have put him, and I will get him." [16]Jesus said to her,

"Mary." She turned toward him and

cried out in Aramaic, "Rabboni!" (which means Teacher).

[17]Jesus said, "Do not hold on to me, for I have not yet

returned to the Father. Go instead to my brothers and tell

them, 'I am returning to my Father and your Father, to my

God and your God.'" [18]Mary Magdalene went to

the disciples with the news: "I have seen the Lord!"

And she told them that he had said these things to her.

(John 20:21-23)

[21]Again Jesus said, "Peace be with you! As the Father has

sent me, I am sending you." [22]And with that he breathed on

them and said, "Receive the Holy Spirit. [23]If you forgive

anyone his sins, they are forgiven;

if you do not forgive them, they are not forgiven."

(John 20:27-28)

[27]Then he said to Thomas, "Put your finger here;

see my hands. Reach out your hand and put it into my side.

그리하고 믿음 없는 자가 되지 말고 믿는 자가 되라

도마가 대답하여 이르되 나의 주님이시며 나의 하나님이시니이다

요한복음 21:13 - 14

예수께서 가셔서 떡을 가져다가 그들에게 주시고

생선도 그와 같이 하시니라

이것은 예수께서 죽은 자 가운데서 살아나신 후에

세 번째로 제자들에게 나타나신 것이라.

*Stop doubting and believe." *[28]*Thomas said to him,*

"My Lord and my God!"

(John 21:13-14)

[13]Jesus came, took the bread and gave it to them,

and did the same with the fish.

[14]This was now the third time Jesus appeared to his disciples

after he was raised from the dead.

6. 지혜에 대한 성구

하나님의 말씀인 성경은 창세기부터 요한계시록에 이르기까지 지혜로 이루어졌다. 그 중 잠언 말씀을 소개하고자 한다.

잠언 1:7

여호와를 경외하는 것이 지식의 근본이어늘

미련한 자는 지혜와 훈계를 멸시하느니라.

잠언 2:6 - 8

대저 여호와는 지혜를 주시며

지식과 명철을 그 입에서 내심이며

그는 정직한 자를 위하여 완전한 지혜를 예비하시며

행실이 온전한 자에게 방패가 되시나니

대저 그는 정의의 길을 보호하시며

그의 성도들의 길을 보전하려 하심이니라.

잠언 2:20 - 22

지혜가 너를 선한 자의 길로 행하게 하며

또 의인의 길을 지키게 하리니 대저 정직한 자는

땅에 거하며 완전한 자는 땅에 남아 있으리라.

그러나 악인은 땅에서 끊어지겠고 간사한 자는 땅에서 뽑히리라.

6. Scriptures on Wisdom

From Genesis to Revelation, the Bible is filled with God's teachings on wisdom. I would like to quote just a few from the book of Proverbs.

(Proverbs 1:7)

⁷The fear of the LORD is the beginning of knowledge,

but fools despise wisdom and discipline.

(Proverbs 2:6-8)

⁶For the LORD gives wisdom, and from his mouth come knowledge and understanding. ⁷He holds victory in store for the upright, he is a shield to those whose walk is blameless,

⁸for he guards the course of the just

and protects the way of his faithful ones.

(Proverbs 2:20-22)

²⁰Thus you will walk in the ways of good men and keep to the paths of the righteous. ²¹For the upright will live in the land, and the blameless will remain in it; ²²but the wicked will be cut off from the land, and the unfaithful will be torn from it.

잠언 3:5 - 7

너는 마음을 다하여 여호와를 신뢰하고

네 명철을 의지하지 말라

너는 범사에 그를 인정하라 그리하면 네 길을 지도하시리라

스스로 지혜롭게 여기지 말지어다.

여호와를 경외하며 악을 떠날지어다.

잠언 3:15 - 18

지혜는 진주보다 귀하니

너의 사모하는 모든 것으로도 이에 비교할 수 없도다

그 오른손에는 장수가 있고 그 왼손에는 부귀가 있나니

그 길은 즐거운 길이요 그의 지름길은 다 평강이니라

지혜는 그 얻은 자에게 생명 나무라 지혜를 가진 자는 복되도다.

잠언 3:25 - 26

너는 갑작스러운 두려움도 악인에게 닥치는 멸망도

두려워하지 말라

대저 여호와는 네가 의지할 자이시라

네 발을 지켜 걸리지 않게 하시리라.

(Proverbs 3:5-7)

[5]*Trust in the* L*ORD* *with all your heart and lean not on your own understanding;* [6]*in all your ways acknowledge him, and he will make your paths straight.* [7]*Do not be wise in your own eyes; fear the* L*ORD* *and shun evil.*

(Proverbs 3:15-18)

[15]*She is more precious than rubies; nothing you desire can compare with her.* [16]*Long life is in her right hand; in her left hand are riches and honor.* [17]*Her ways are pleasant ways, and all her paths are peace.* [18]*She is a tree of life to those who embrace her; those who lay hold of her will be blessed.*

(Here, wisdom is personified as "she." *Editor's note.*)

(Proverbs 3:25-26)

[25]*Have no fear of sudden disaster or of the ruin that overtakes the wicked,*

[26]*for the* L*ORD* *will be your confidence and will keep your foot from being snared.*

잠언 7:4 - 5

지혜에게 너는 내 누이라 하며

명철에게 너는 내 친족이라 하라

그리하면 이것이 너를 지켜서 음녀에게

말로 호리는 이방 여인에게 빠지지 않게 하리라.

잠언 8:12 - 13

나 지혜는 명철로 주소를 삼으며 지식과 근신을 찾아 얻나니

여호와를 경외하는 것은 악을 미워하는 것이라

나는 교만과 거만과 악한 행실과 패역한 입을 미워하느니라.

잠언 9:10

여호와를 경외하는 것이 지혜의 근본이요

거룩하신 자를 아는 것이 명철이니라.

잠언 10:1

솔로몬의 잠언이라 지혜로운 아들은 아비를 기쁘게 하거니와

미련한 아들은 어미의 근심이니라.

잠언 10:14

지혜로운 자는 지식을 간직하거니와

미련한 자의 입은 멸망에 가까우니라.

(Proverbs 7:4-5)

⁴*Say to wisdom, "You are my sister," and call understanding*

your kinsman;

⁵*they will keep you from the adulteress,*

from the wayward wife with her seductive words.

(Proverbs 8:12-13)

¹² *"I, wisdom, dwell together with prudence; I possess knowledge*

and discretion. ¹³*To fear the LORD is to hate evil; I hate pride and*

arrogance, evil behavior and perverse speech."

(Proverbs 9:10)

¹⁰*The fear of the LORD is the beginning of wisdom,*

and knowledge of the Holy One is understanding.

(Proverbs 10:1)

¹*The proverbs of Solomon: A wise son brings joy to his father,*

but a foolish son grief to his mother.

(Proverbs 10:14)

¹⁴*Wise men store up knowledge,*

but the mouth of a fool invites ruin.

잠언 10:23

미련한 자는 행악으로 낙을 삼는 것같이

명철한 자는 지혜로 낙을 삼느니라.

잠언 10:29

여호와의 도가 정직한 자에게는 산성이요

행악하는 자에게는 멸망이니라.

잠언 11:2

교만이 오면 욕도 오거니와 겸손한 자에게는 지혜가 있느니라.

잠언 11:12

지혜 없는 자는 그의 이웃을 멸시하나 명철한 자는 잠잠하느니라.

잠언 12:4

어진 여인은 그 지아비의 면류관이나

욕을 끼치는 여인은 그 지아비의 뼈가 썩음 같게 하느니라.

잠언 13:1

지혜로운 아들은 아비의 훈계를 들으나

거만한 자는 꾸지람을 즐겨 듣지 아니하느니라.

(Proverbs 10:23)

[23]*A fool finds pleasure in evil conduct,*

but a man of understanding delights in wisdom.

(Proverbs 10:29)

[29]*The way of the LORD is a refuge for the righteous,*

but it is the ruin of those who do evil.

(Proverbs 11:2)

[2]*When pride comes, then comes disgrace,*

but with humility comes wisdom.

(Proverbs 11:12)

[12]*A man who lacks judgment derides his neighbor,*

but a man of understanding holds his tongue.

(Proverbs 12:4)

[4]*A wife of noble character is her husband's crown,*

but a disgraceful wife is like decay in his bones.

(Proverbs 13:1)

[1]*A wise son heeds his father's instruction,*

but a mocker does not listen to rebuke.

잠언 13:14

지혜 있는 자의 교훈은 생명의 샘이니
사람으로 사망의 그물을 벗어나게 하느니라.

잠언 13:20

지혜로운 자와 동행하면 지혜를 얻고
미련한 자와 사귀면 해를 받느니라.

잠언 14:1

지혜로운 여인은 자기 집을 세우되
미련한 여인은 자기 손으로 그것을 허느니라.

잠언 15:1 - 2

유순한 대답은 분노를 쉬게 하여도
말은 노를 격동하느니라
지혜 있는 자의 혀는 지식을 선히 베풀고
미련한 자의 입은 미련한 것을 쏟느니라.

잠언 24:3 - 4

집은 지혜로 말미암아 건축되고 명철로 말미암아
견고하게 되며 또 방들은 지식으로 말미암아
각종 귀하고 아름다운 보배로 채우게 되느니라.

(Proverbs 13:14)

[14]*The teaching of the wise is a fountain of life,*

turning a man from the snares of death.

(Proverbs 13:20)

[20]*He who walks with the wise grows wise,*

but a companion of fools suffers harm.

(Proverbs 14:1)

[1]*The wise woman builds her house,*

but with her own hands the foolish one tears hers down.

(Proverbs 15:1-2)

[1]*A gentle answer turns away wrath, but a harsh word stirs up*
anger. [2]*The tongue of the wise commends knowledge, but the*
mouth of the fool gushes folly.

(Proverbs 24:3-4)

[3]*By wisdom a house is built, and through understanding it is*
established; [4]*through knowledge its*
rooms are filled with rare and beautiful treasures.

잠언 25:21

네 원수가 배고파하거든 음식을 먹이고

목말라하거든 물을 마시게 하라.

잠언 31:30 - 31

고운 것도 거짓되고 아름다운 것도 헛되나

오직 여호와를 경외하는 여자는 칭찬을 받을 것이라

그 손의 열매가 그에게로 돌아갈 것이요

그 행한 일로 말미암아 성문에서 칭찬을 받으리라.

(Proverbs 25:21)

²¹*If your enemy is hungry, give him food to eat;*

if he is thirsty, give him water to drink.

(Proverbs 31:30-31)

³⁰*Charm is deceptive, and beauty is fleeting;*

*but a woman who fears the L*ORD *is to be praised.*

³¹*Give her the reward she has earned,*

and let her works bring her praise at the city gate.

7. 복에 대한 성구

　세상은 돈 많고 자녀 많고 건강하면 복이 있다고 한다. 성경은 삼위일체 되시는 하나님을 경외하는 자가 복 있는 자라고 가르친다. 예수 그리스도를 믿고 하나님의 말씀을 순종하여, 살아계신 하나님께서 인정하시고 기뻐하시는 복 있는 자가 되시기를 기원한다.

시편 1편

복 있는 사람은 악인들의 꾀를 따르지 아니하며

죄인들의 길에 서지 아니하며

오만한 자들의 자리에 앉지 아니하고

오직 여호와의 율법을 즐거워하여

그의 율법을 주야로 묵상하는도다

그는 시냇가에 심은 나무가 철을 따라 열매를 맺으며

그 잎사귀가 마르지 아니함 같으니

그가 하는 모든 일이 다 형통하리로다

악인들은 그렇지 아니함이여

오직 바람에 나는 겨와 같도다.

그러므로 악인들은 심판을 견디지 못하며

죄인들이 의인들의 모임에 들지 못하리로다

7. Scriptures on Blessings

We are said to be blessed, in worldly eyes, if we have wealth, many children, and good health. But the Bible teaches us that blessed is he who stands in awe of God. I pray that you will believe in Christ, obey the Word of God, and become blessed people, pleasing in God's eyes.

(Psalm 1)
[1]Blessed is the man who does not walk in
the counsel of the wicked or stand in the way of sinners or sit
in the seat of mockers.
[2]But his delight is in the law of the Lord,
and on his law he meditates day and night.
[3]He is like a tree planted by streams of water,
which yields its fruit in season
and whose leaf does not wither.
Whatever he does prospers.
[4]Not so the wicked!
They are like chaff that the wind blows away.
[5]Therefore the wicked will not stand in the judgment,
nor sinners in the assembly of the righteous.

무릇 의인들의 길은 여호와께서 인정하시나
악인들의 길은 망하리로다.

시편 32:1
허물의 사함을 받고 자신의 죄가 가려진 자는 복이 있도다.

시편 37:22
주의 복을 받은 자들은 땅을 차지하고
주의 저주를 받은 자들은 끊어지리로다.

시편 37:25 - 26
내가 어려서부터 늙기까지 의인이 버림을 당하거나
그의 자손이 걸식함을 보지 못하였도다
그는 종일토록 은혜를 베풀고 꾸어주니
그의 자손이 복을 받는도다.

시편 40:4
여호와를 의지하고
교만한 자와 거짓에 치우치는 자를
돌아보지 아니하는 자는 복이 있도다.

*⁶For the L*ORD *watches over the way of the righteous,*
but the way of the wicked will perish.

(Psalm 32:1)
¹Blessed is he whose transgressions are forgiven,
whose sins are covered.

(Psalm 37:22)
*²²Those the L*ORD *blesses will inherit the land,*
but those he curses will be cut off.

(Psalm 37:25-26)
²⁵I was young and now I am old, yet I have never seen the
righteous forsaken or their children begging bread.
²⁶They are always generous and lend freely;
their children will be blessed.

(Psalm 40:4)
*⁴Blessed is the man who makes the L*ORD *his trust,*
who does not look to the proud,
to those who turn aside to false gods.

시편 67:1 - 7

하나님은 우리에게 은혜를 베푸사 복을 주시고

그의 얼굴 빛을 우리에게 비취사 주의 도를 땅 위에

주의 구원을 모든 나라에게 알리소서

하나님이여 민족들이 주를 찬송하게 하시며

모든 민족들이 주를 찬송하게 하소서

온 백성은 기쁘고 즐겁게 노래할지니

주는 민족들을 공평히 심판하시며

땅 위의 나라들을 다스리실 것임이니이다

하나님이여 민족들이 주를 찬송하게 하시며

모든 민족으로 주를 찬송하게 하소서

땅이 그의 소산을 내어주었으니

하나님 곧 우리 하나님이 우리에게 복을 주시리로다

하나님이 우리에게 복을 주시리니

땅의 모든 끝이 하나님을 경외하리로다.

시편 84:4 - 5

주의 집에 사는 자들은 복이 있나니

그들이 항상 주를 찬송하리이다

주께 힘을 얻고 그 마음에 시온의 대로가 있는 자는 복이 있나이다.

(Psalm 67:1-7)

[1]May God be gracious to us and bless us

and make his face shine upon us,

[2]that your ways may be known on earth,

your salvation among all nations.

[3]May the peoples praise you, O God;

may all the peoples praise you.

[4]May the nations be glad and sing for joy,

for you rule the peoples justly

and guide the nations of the earth.

[5]May the peoples praise you, O God;

may all the peoples praise you.

[6]Then the land will yield its harvest,

God, our God, will bless us. [7]God will bless us,

and all the ends of the earth will fear him.

(Psalm 84:4-5)

[4]Blessed are those who dwell in your house;

they are ever praising you. [5]Blessed are those whose strength

is in you, who have set their hearts on pilgrimage.

시편 84:10 - 12

주의 궁정에서의 한 날이 다른 곳에서의 천 날보다 나은 즉

악인의 장막에 사는 것보다 내 하나님의 성전 문지기로

있는 것이 좋사오니 여호와 하나님은 해요 방패이시라

여호와께서 은혜와 영화를 주시며

정직히 행하는 자에게 좋은 것을 아끼지 아니하실 것임이니이다

만군의 여호와여 주께 의지하는 자는 복이 있나이다.

시편 112:1

할렐루야 여호와를 경외하며

그의 계명을 크게 즐거워하는 자는 복이 있도다.

시편 134:1 - 3

보라 밤에 여호와의 성전에 서 있는 여호와의 모든 종들아

여호와를 송축하라

성소를 향하여 너희 손을 들고 여호와를 송축하라

천지를 지으신 여호와께서 시온에서 네게 복을 주실지어다.

잠언 22:9

선한 눈을 가진 자는 복을 받으리니

이는 양식을 가난한 자에게 줌이니라.

(Psalm 84:10-12)

[10]*Better is one day in your courts than a thousand elsewhere; I would rather be a doorkeeper in the house of my God than dwell in the tents of the wicked.* [11]*For the L*ORD *God is a sun and shield; the L*ORD *bestows favor and honor; no good thing does he withhold from those whose walk is blameless.*
[12]*O L*ORD *Almighty, blessed is the man who trusts in you.*

(Psalm 112:1)

[1]*Praise the L*ORD*. Blessed is the man who fears the L*ORD*, who finds great delight in his commands.*

(Psalm 134:1-3)

[1]*Praise the L*ORD*, all you servants of the L*ORD *who minister by night in the house of the L*ORD*.* [2]*Lift up your hands in the sanctuary and praise the L*ORD*.* [3]*May the L*ORD*, the Maker of heaven and earth, bless you from Zion.*

(Proverbs 22:9)

[9]*A generous man will himself be blessed, for he shares his food with the poor.*

심령이 가난한 자는 복이 있나니 천국이 그들의 것임이요

애통하는 자는 복이 있나니 그들이 위로를 받을 것임이요

온유한 자는 복이 있나니 그들이 땅을 기업으로 받을 것임이요

의에 주리고 목마른 자는 복이 있나니 그들이 배부를 것임이요

긍휼히 여기는 자는 복이 있나니

그들이 긍휼히 여김을 받을 것임이요

마음이 청결한 자는 복이 있나니 그들이 하나님을 볼 것임이요

화평하게 하는 자는 복이 있나니

그들이 하나님의 아들이라 일컬음을 받을 것임이요

의를 위하여 박해를 받은 자는 복이 있나니

천국이 그들의 것임이라

나로 말미암아 너희를 욕하고 박해하고

거짓으로 너희를 거슬러 모든 악한 말을 할 때에는

너희에게 복이 있나니 기뻐하고 즐거워하라

하늘에서 너희의 상이 큼이라

너희 전에 있던 선지자들도 이같이 박해하였느니라.

(Matthew 5:3-12)

[3] *"Blessed are the poor in spirit, for theirs is the kingdom of heaven.* [4] *Blessed are those who mourn, for they will be comforted.* [5] *Blessed are the meek, for they will inherit the earth.* [6] *Blessed are those who hunger and thirst for righteousness, for they will be filled.* [7] *Blessed are the merciful, for they will be shown mercy.* [8] *Blessed are the pure in heart, for they will see God.* [9] *Blessed are the peacemakers, for they will be called sons of God.* [10] *Blessed are those who are persecuted because of righteousness, for theirs is the kingdom of heaven.* [11] *Blessed are you when people insult you, persecute you and falsely say all kinds of evil against you because of me.* [12] *Rejoice and be glad, because great is your reward in heaven, for in the same way they persecuted the prophets who were before you."*

Chapter 6

*Temperance is the
Fruit of the Holy Spirit*

절제는
성령의 열매

제26회 절제회 총회
The 26th KWCTU Convention (1989)

술과 담배 해독 일깨우는 청소년 절제회
웅변대회
Speech Contest to inform of the
harms of alcohol and nicotine (1993)

대한기독교여자절제회 60주년 총회
The 60th anniversary of the KWCTU (1983)

1991년 6월 26일 세계절제회 회장 미니 롤린스 방문
Visit by World WCTU President Minnie Rawlins (June 26, 1991)

2003년 5월 10일 연세대학교 축제기간 절제 캠페인
Temperance campaigns at Yonsei University (May 10, 2003)

2004년 9월 9일 FAS Seminar: 태아알콜 중독 증후군 예방 세미나
Fetal Alcohol Syndrome (FAS) Prevention Seminar (September 9, 2004)

1. 인류를 술에서 구원하자

술이란 마약이 언제부터 인간의 생명을 사망으로 이끌어 가게 되었는지 우리는 이 한탄스러운 사실을 알 수가 없다. 온 인류가 지금 술과 마약으로 인하여 죄에서 허덕이고 있다. 젊은이들은 마리화나를 피우며 일시적이나마 모든 괴로움에서 벗어나 짧은 쾌감으로 자기의 인격과 건강을 파괴하고 있다.

우리 인간 사회에서 술은 마귀의 큰 유혹의 도구임을 기억하자. 하와 할머니가 선악과를 따먹게 한 이후 마귀는 인류를 사망의 구렁텅이로 이끌어 가는데 술을 가장 큰 무기의 하나로 쓰고 있다. 술을 마시면 간음죄를 범하게 된다. 간음죄를 범하는 자는 하나님의 저주를 받게 된다. 간음죄를 범하는 곳에는 많은 성병이 무섭게 도사리고 있다. 이러한 병을 가진 자는 완전한 자녀를 낳을 수가 없다. 술에 취해서 임신된 아이도 마찬가지다. 얼마나 많은 정신병자가 일어나고 있는가! 부모가 술을 먹고 낳은 자, 성병이 있는 부모가 낳은 자, 그리고 성병을 치료하면서 강한 항생제를 먹는 중에 임신 된 자 등은 지진아로 태어나게 된다. 그 결과 지금 세계 각국의 정신병원은 초만원이며 심지어 여러 국가에서는 이들 정신병자를 다 수용할 수 없어서 방치하고 있는 실정이어서, 일반 시민들의 가정에 많은 피해가 일어나고 있다는 보도이다.

1. Let Us Save Humanity from Alcohol

We do not know since when the addiction to alcohol became so prevalent in our society, dragging countless people towards death. Humanity is being tormented by alcohol and drugs. Young people are smoking marijuana and forgoing both their human dignity and health, all for a momentary escape from worries or a brief adventurous sensation.

Let us be reminded that alcohol is one of Satan's biggest instruments of temptation in our society today. Satan's first form of temptation led Eve to eat the fruit of the knowledge of good and evil, and now, Satan is using alcohol to bring humanity down to the pits of eternal condemnation in the dark. When we drink alcohol, we open ourselves up to commit sins such as adultery. Those who commit adultery condemn themselves. Adultery cultivates many serious health hazards such as STDs (Sexually Transmitted Diseases). And those who contract STDs cannot bear healthy children. Likewise, children born of alcoholic mothers are not healthy. Oh, how quickly the number of children born with defects is rising! Children born to mothers who drink while pregnant or who have STDs and take antibiotics during pregnancy are usually born with mental disabilities. Mental hospitals around the world are becoming overcrowded with more and more people. So many countries lack the capacity to care for such

　술이란 적당히 마시면 좋다는 억설을 주류업자들에게 연구비를 받은 학자들이 프랑스 포도주 판촉을 위해 퍼뜨리고 있다. 그런데 이 말을 믿고 너도나도 술을 마시고 있다. 나는 예언한다. 장차 인류는 술로 말미암아 큰 저주의 구렁텅이로 빠질 것이다. 이 무서운 술에서 우리 인류가 구원 받으려면 힘을 다해 모든 정신을 차려서 무서운 사단의 올무에서 헤쳐 나와야 하겠다.

patients. And the people who suffer most from such problems are innocent families.

The idea that moderate drinking of alcohol is good for your health is spread by researchers who have been paid by brewing companies in a scheme to increase wine sales. And believing such deceitful words, people are choosing to drink alcoholic beverages. I foresee humanity condemning itself deeper and deeper into the grave through alcohol intake. In order for humanity to be saved from this lethal substance called alcohol, we must all think straight and jump out of Satan's tangled net of temptation.

2. 지혜로운 여성이 되자

대한민국에 절제회가 창설된 지 50주년을 맞이하여 감사한 마음을 다 표현하기 어렵습니다. 돌이켜 보건대 절제운동은 애국 운동이라 일제 탄압으로 잠시 중단되었다가 해방과 더불어 다시 시작되었습니다. 회관이 없어 여러 가지 어려운 운영을 거듭하던 중 하나님의 도우심으로 이제 우리는 절제운동을 할 수 있는 터전을 마련하게 됨을 감사히 생각합니다.

한 나라가 흥하고 패함에는 그 민족정신에 좌우됨을 재론할 필요도 없습니다. 특히 민족을 기르는 여성들이 지혜로운 여성이 될 때 그 민족은 얼마나 행복한 나라를 이루겠습니까? 지혜로운 여성이란 모든 일에 절제하여야 합니다.

첫째, 시간을 절제하여야 합니다. 시간이란 곧 생명입니다. 인생이란 내일을 아무도 보장하지 못합니다. 과거를 논하고 과거를 사랑하는 것도 허무합니다. 지금 사는 이 시간이 곧 삶의 시간으로 하나님이 주신 선물입니다. 이 귀중한 시간을 절제하며 소중히 아껴 사는 사람이 곧 지혜로운 사람입니다. 앞으로 우리 민족이 정확하고 신속한 시간관념으로 세계 역사에 남도록 시간을 소중히 아끼며 사는 민족이 되어야 하겠습니다.

둘째로, 말의 허물이 없는 자는 온전한 자라고 성경에 말씀하셨습니다. 인간은 궁정 안 용상에 누운 임금으로부터 길바

2. Let Us Become Wise Women
Commemoration Message on the 50th Anniversary of the KWCTU (September 1973)

It is hard for me to express my gratitude in its entirety at this 50th anniversary celebration of the KWCTU. The KWCTU was banned for years under Japanese suppression of all national movements. I thank God for His presence throughout the past fifty years of hardship and challenges we faced by not having a permanent meeting place. I thank Him, for He surely provided us with a hall for the KWCTU.

It is unquestionable that a people's level of national consciousness determines the country's steps toward prosperity or defeat. If mothers and women, in general, become wise, how much more joy and happiness would the entire nation experience? Wise women should be temperate in all things.

First, we should exercise temperance in the use of time. Life is basically time—if one stops, the other stops also. Life never guarantees tomorrow. The act of reminiscing upon the past and yearning to travel back in time is hopeless. Those who practice temperance of His precious gift of time are truly wise. I urge all people of this nation to practice temperance in the use of time and thus go down in history.

Second, the Bible says that a righteous man is faultless

닥에 누운 거지까지도 다 하나님의 피조물로 소중한 생명입니다. 이 귀한 생명을 어느 누가 비난할 수 있으며, 비난할 권리가 있습니까 성경에 미련한 자라도 잠잠하면 지혜로운 자로 보인다고 하였습니다. 짧은 인생 길에 서로의 인격을 소중히 여기며 서로를 사랑하며 사는 지혜로운 여성이 많아지면 우리 사회는 얼마나 행복하겠습니까?

셋째로, 물질의 절제입니다. 한 사람이 건강하려면 육체에 필요한 혈관이 정상적으로 순환 되어야 하는 것과 같이, 한 나라가 흥함에는 물질의 유통이 잘 되어야 발전이 따라옵니다. 간단히 말해서 물질은 내 겨레의 피임을 생각하고 한 푼을 쓸 때도 정신을 똑바로 차려서 사용하는 지혜로운 여성이 되어야 하겠습니다.

이제 국가의 기초석이 되는 절제 정신이 우리 민족의 가슴 가슴마다 심어질 때 우리 겨레의 앞날은 영광과 번영으로 빛날 것을 믿습니다. 위로 조물주 되시는 하나님을 신봉하고 아래로 내 조국을 사랑하는 마음과 국가의 기초석이 되는 절제 정신이 내 가족으로부터 내 이웃, 친척, 친구, 온 겨레에게 다 퍼질 때 하나님은 우리 겨레에게 복음 내리셔서 이제까지는 다른 나라의 도움을 받는 생활 상태에서 벗어나 우리도 이웃 나라를 도울 수 있는 부유한 나라로 성장할 것을 확신합니다.

with his choice of words. All people are God's beloved creation—from the enthroned king in a palace to a beggar on the streets, we are all His people. Who can place blame or be the judge of anyone's life? The Bible indicates that even foolish men who remain quiet show wisdom. How much happier would life be if the world were filled with more wise women who live with love and compassion for others throughout this short journey of life?

Third, temperance should be exercised in the acquirement of material possessions. In the way that blood must flow in the right direction and with the right pressure in order for the body to function, sound circulation of money and resources must be maintained for a country to develop. In other words, we must consider our money our nation's blood, and spend it wisely.

When the spirit of the temperance movement, which is the rock of the nation, becomes planted in every person's heart, I believe the future of our nation will shine with glory and prosperity. When we put our faith in the God of all creation and when, with a loving heart for our nation, the spirit of the temperance movement spreads to our families, relatives, and neighbors, God will give our nation His blessings. Our nation has thus far been at the receiving end of foreign aid, but I

　끝으로, 내 한 생명이 피를 흘려 이 민족이 잘 된다면 누가 그 생명을 아끼겠습니까? 절제 운동을 한다는 것은 내 생명을 바치는 것보다 용이한 일이니 내 정열을 다 바쳐도 아깝지 아니한 이 귀한 운동에 우리 다 함께 참여합시다. 감사합니다.

(1973년 9월 절제회 50주년 기념사)

trust that God will raise our nation to be at the helping end.

Who wouldn't spare one's own life if only one's nation could prosper through the shedding of one's own blood? Let us recognize how precious the spreading of the temperance movement is and bring our wholehearted efforts to the movement. Thank you.

Chapter 7
Praise the Lord
하나님을
찬양하라

28차 세계기독교여자절제대회에서 독창
My solo at the 28th World Convention in
Sheffield, England (1980)

65회 생신
On my 65th birthday (1983)

1983년 밴프호텔 엘리자베스 여왕
기념실
At the Queen Elizabeth Hall in
Banff, Canada

절제회 설교
Preaching at the KWCTU Hall (1977)

서울 34차 세계절제대회 설교하는 김영훈 대성그룹 회장
The Daesung Group Chairman Younghoon David Kim, delivering a sermon at the 34th World Convention of the WWCTU held in Seoul, Korea (1998)

34차 세계절제대회에서 둘째 딸과
With his daughter at the 34th World Convention in Seoul, Korea (1998)

육사 국궁장에서 아들에게 국궁 지도
Teaching his son Korean archery (2001)

이사야 35:1 - 4

광야와 메마른 땅이 기뻐하며

사막이 백합화같이 피어 즐거워하며

무성하게 피어 기쁜 노래로 즐거워하며

레바논의 영광과 갈멜과 사론의 아름다움을 얻을 것이라

그것들이 여호와의 영광 곧 우리 하나님의 아름다움을 보리로다

너희는 약한 손을 강하게 하여 주며 떨리는 무릎을 굳게 하여주며

겁내는 자에게 이르기를 너는 굳세어라 두려워 말라

보라 너희 하나님이 오사 보복하시며 갚아 주실 것이라

하나님이 오사 너희를 구하시리라 하라

빌라도 뜰에 선 주님

빌라도 뜰에 서신 죄 없는 우리 주님
제사장 율법사들 모두 다 살기 등등
두려워 어찌할까 모르니까 그렇지

지금도 주님 길을 바르게 따르려면
험한 산 악마들에 시험도 많더란다
아무리 어려웁지만 이기고도 남으리

Poems by the Author

Isaiah 35:1-4

*¹ The desert and the parched land will be glad;
the wilderness will rejoice and blossom. Like the crocus,
it will burst into bloom; ²it will rejoice greatly and shout
for joy. The glory of Lebanon will be given to it, the splendor
of Carmel and Sharon; they will see the glory of the Lord,
the splendor of our God. ³Strengthen the feeble hands,
steady the knees that give way; ⁴say to those with fearful
hearts, "Be strong, do not fear; your God will come,
he will come with vengeance; with divine retribution
he will come to save you."*

The Lord in Pilate's Yard

*(Written on Thursday, Holy Week, March 26, 1970, when the KWCTU Hall
was being built)*

Our innocent Lord stands in Pilate's yard,
And the bloodthirsty chief priests and elders
Hide in fear of the Lord.

The way of the Lord is paved with Many rough
mountains and great temptations. But no matter the

제자들 가버리고 혼자 선 그 모습은
얼마나 외로우며 고독에 잠겼을까
아무리 외로웁지만 주님보다 더하리

(1970년 3월 26일 수난 주간 목요일 절제회관 건축 도중)

부활과 승리

주님은 무덤에서 일찍이 살아나서
따르던 제자보다 앞서서 갈릴리로
가시며 하신 말씀 안부하라 하셨네

우리도 주님 가신 그 길을 따르면
주께서 승리하신 그 부활 참여하리
믿고서 힘차게 살아 주와 같이 되려네

하나님 우편에는 주님이 앉아 계셔
지금도 우리 위해 간절히 구하시며
우리의 허물 보시고 용서하라 하시네

우리도 주님 보좌 그곳에 같이 앉아
세상에 살던 설움 하소연 드리면
주님의 못 자국 손이 내 마음을 달래리!

(절제회관 건축 중 1970년 3월 27일 성 금요일)

trials and tribulations, we will be victorious.
When the Lord's disciples deserted Him, leaving Him
all alone, Oh, how lonely He must have been!
We may feel desolate at times, yet never more than
the Lord.

Revival and Victory

*(Written on Good Friday, March 27, 1970, when the KWCTU Hall
was being built)*

Christ arose from the grave,
Walked to the Sea of Galilee ahead of His disciples,
And said to them, "Peace be with you."

When we follow the path of Christ,
We too can join in the victory of His resurrection.
Living boldly in faith, I want to be more like Christ.

Christ is seated at the right hand of God.
Even now, His ardent prayers are with us;
He looks at our mistakes and commands forgiveness.

We will also sit at the throne of Christ.
And when we present our grievances
and worldly hardships,
The nail-scarred hands of Christ will comfort
our hearts.

이사야 40:30 - 31
소년이라도 피곤하며 곤비하며
장정이라도 넘어지며 쓰러지되
오직 여호와를 앙망하는 자는 새 힘을 얻으리니
독수리의 날개치며 올라감 같을 것이요
달음박질하여도 곤비하지 아니하겠고
걸어가도 피곤하지 아니하리로다

조국

내 조국 없이 살던 일제 때 쓰라림은
아무리 잊으려 해도 잊히질 않지요
내 조국 도로 찾아서 내 무엇을 하였지

내 조국 바로 세울 한 조각 돌이 되어
청춘의 한 맺혔던 선배들 혼들께도
내 조국 도로 찾아서 내 무엇을 바쳤지

한 번 오가는 인생 너무들 비겁말고
하루를 살다 가도 내 조국 기초석 되어
천당에 가서라도 후회함이 없이 살자

(1972년 1월 19일)

Isaiah 40:30-31

[30]*Even youths grow tired and weary,*

and young men stumble and fall;

[31]*but those who hope in*

the LORD will renew their strength.

They will soar on wings like eagles;

they will run and not grow weary,

they will walk and not be faint.

My Country

(January 19, 1972)

The pain of countrylessness and hardship under
Japanese occupation,
These things I try to forget but cannot.
Reclaiming my country, what did I do to help?

Becoming a pebble of stone for my country
And for the begrudging souls of my seniors,
Reclaiming my country, what else did I dedicate?

We only have one life to live—let us not be cowardly.
Even if I should only live a single day,
I will become the bedrock of my country
And live a life I will not regret when I am in heaven.

부활의 소망

죽음이 다가온들 두려움 어디 있나
숨지면 내 영혼은 하늘의 영광 앞에
어엿이 다시 살아나 우리 주님 만나리

부활은 인생 길의 광명한 소망이라
이 소망 가진 자는 더 무엇 바라리요
인생 길 맑게 살다 흠이 없이 가려네

그때 의인들은 자기 아버지 나라에서
해와 같이 빛나리라 귀 있는 자는 들으라

(마태복음 13:43) (1972년 1월 11일)

Hope of Resurrection

(January 11, 1972)

What is there to fear in approaching death?
My breathless soul will revive again before
The glory of heaven and will meet my Lord.

Resurrection is the bright hope of life's journey.
What else could those who have this hope possibly
ask for? I want to live a life holy, righteous, and
blameless before Him.

For it is written: *Then the righteous will shine like
the sun in the kingdom of their Father. He who has
ears, let him hear. (Matthew 13:43)*

승리 민족

우리는 이 나라의 하나의 벽돌이요
우리의 손에 든 돈 내 겨레의 피랍니다
이 재물 소중히 여겨 승리 민족 되리다

경제가 넘어지면 나라도 없어지고
나라가 없어지면 민족도 흩어지네
우리는 단결하여서 내 겨레의 힘 되자

먼저 간 선진들은 내 조국 찾으려고
피 흘려 순교하며 왜놈의 모진 학대
맨주먹 쥐고 막았네 승리 민족 되려고

우리는 하나님의 귀하신 자녀이며
우리는 하나님의 곡간을 맡아보는
충성된 청지기라네

(1971년 11월)

Victorious Nation

(November 1971)

We are the bricks of this nation.
The money we hold in our hands comes
from the blood of our brothers.
Cherish this treasure and become a victorious nation.

If the economy falls, the nation disappears;
If the nation disappears, its peoples scatter about.
Unite in solidarity and become our nation's strength.

Our ancestors sacrificed their blood to martyrdom
And blocked cruel foreign treatment with their bare fists,
All to reclaim this nation and to make it victorious.

We are the precious children of God.
We have been called to be faithful stewards
in the household of God and to live
With fear and trembling before Him.

노래로

노래로 일어나서 노래로 밥을 짓고
노래로 아기 젖을 먹이던 그 옛날에
새까만 작은 눈들이 이렇게도 자랐네

(1970년 3월 26일)

에스더

꿈에도 그리워라 어머님 무릎 위에
젖 먹던 시절에는 에스더같아여라
수시로 축복하시던 그리우신 그 음성
에스더같이 되게 이 마음 다짐했지
나 언제 어머니 되어 내 애기 젖 먹이며
우리 딸 에스더같이 되기 위해 빌었네

(1971년 7월 19일 아침)

With Song

(March 26, 1970)

Long ago, I woke up with song, cooked with song,
And fed my babies with song.
And now their little black beady eyes have grown.

Esther

(Morning of July 19, 1971)

I miss my mother even in my dreams.
I miss hearing her voice telling me
To become like Esther,
As she fed me on her lap.
I pledged my heart to become like Esther.
And when I became a mother, I prayed that
My daughter too would become like Esther,
As I fed her on my lap.

장미

분홍 빛 노랑 장미 방긋이 피웠구나
이슬로 세수하여 너의 잎 진주 구슬
한 송이 따다 꽂아 마루에 향내 내고
두 송이 따다 꽂아 방안에 향기 내네
오늘도 꽃바구니를 님 타시는 차 안에

(1969년 5월)

창조의 신비

하늘은 그 영광을 장엄히 찬양하네
땅 위에 화초들은 찬란히 빛나누나
피조물 우리 인생도 그 은혜에 감사해
밤이면 무수한 별 이 마음 황홀하고
낮이면 저 밝은 빛 이 세상 비추이니
이 조화 무궁한 은사 우리 마음 감격해

(1972년 봄)

Roses

(May 1969)

I see the pink and yellow roses have bloomed.

I see the morning dew has left pearl-like beads on
their leaves.

Pick one stem of rose to fill the living room with a
sweet aroma;

Pick two more to fill the bedroom with this sweet
aroma.

Today as always I place a basket of flowers in my
dear husband's car.

The Mystery of Creation

(Spring 1972)

The skies grandly praise your glory;

Gardens shine brightly.

All creation gives thanks for His grace.

The countless stars in the evening sky charm our hearts;

The bright daylight illuminates the entire world.

This eternal gift of creation's harmony moves our hearts.

일어나라, 빛을 발하라

김영훈 대성그룹 회장

제 34회 WWCTU 세계 대회 설교

1998년 5월 10일

기도

사랑하는 주님,

오늘은 34회 세계 대회의 만찬이 열리는 세계 대회의 마지막 날입니다. 세계 기독교 여자 절제회의 대표들과 함께 크리스천으로서 21세기를 어떻게 준비할 지에 대해 저에게 주셨던 묵상을 나눌 수 있는 기회를 주심을 감사드립니다. 당신의 은혜와 진리로 우리의 마음이 채워질 수 있도록, 주님의 성령으로 우리 모두의 마음을 가득 채워주소서. 예수님의 이름으로 기도드립니다. 아멘.

Arise and Shine!

(Sermon by Younghoon David Kim at the 34th Triennial World Convention of the WWCTU, May 10, 1988)

Prayer:

Loving Father,

Today we have gathered at the banquet on this last day of the 34th World Convention of the WWCTU. Thank you for giving me this blessed opportunity to share with worldwide WCTU delegates and members what you revealed to me about how we, as Christians, must prepare for the 21st century. I ask that you fill our hearts with Your Holy Spirit so that our hearts may overflow with Your grace and Truth. In the name of Jesus Christ our Lord, I pray. Amen.

1. 서론

　　오늘은 세계 대회의 마지막 날입니다. 오순절날 성령이 제자들에게 권능으로 임했던 것 같이, 오늘 이 곳에 모인 모든 분들께도 성령의 풍성한 기름 부으심이 함께 하시기를 기도합니다. 이렇게 중요한 오늘 같은 날, 믿음의 본질적인 요소들에 대해 보다 자세히 들여다보는 것은 우리에게 아주 의미 있는 일일 것입니다. 최근, 정치, 경제와 사회 영역의 위기들로 인해 사회의 모든 부분에 아주 많은 고난과 어려움들이 있습니다. 예컨대, 현재 IMF 체제 하의 한국의 경제 상황은 한국 전쟁 기간보다도 더 힘든 상황으로 여겨지기도 합니다. 왜냐하면 한국 전쟁 기간 동안은 남측에 피난처라도 있었기 때문입니다. 특별히 WWCTU의 기독여성들이 성경은 어려움과 위기의 순간 우리에게 무엇이라 말하고 있는지 새롭게 찾아보는 것은 아주 의미 있는 일입니다. 그러기 위해서 기독인의 세 가지 본질적인 삶의 모습에 대해 다시 한번 생각해 보아야 할 것입니다.

　　첫째, 성령 충만한 기독 여성의 특징은 무엇인가?
　　둘째, 어떻게 기독 여성들이 세계를 정복할 것인가?
　　셋째, 어떻게 기독 여성들 특히 WWCTU가 하나님 나라 확장에 쓰임을 받을 것인가?

　　이 세 가지 질문에 대답하기 위해 룻기에 나오는 말씀들을 함께 살펴보겠습니다.

1. Introduction

Today is the last day of the World Convention of the WWCTU. I pray that God will anoint each and every one of you here with the fullness of His Holy Spirit, just as the Holy Spirit was with Jesus' disciples at Pentecost. On such a significant day as this, I feel it is very suitable for us to look deeply into the essential elements of our faith. The current political, economic, and social state of disorder has fostered great trials and tribulations around the world. For example, the economic situation in Korea under the IMF may be considered worse than it was during the Korean War. At least during the Korean War, our people were able to seek refuge in the south. But there's no hiding from the IMF. It is important for Christians today, especially Christian women of the WCTU, to learn anew what the bible teaches about facing hardship and crisis. We will examine three questions about the Christian walk of faith.

- What are the characteristics of a Christian woman who is filled with the Holy Spirit?
- How will Christian women conquer the world?
- How will the WWCTU be used to expand the kingdom of God?

Let us turn to the Book of Ruth to find God's answer to these questions.

2. 본론

(1) 성경적인 여성: 속사람이 강건한 여성

성경 속에는 많은 믿음의 여성들이 등장합니다. 특별히 잠언 31장은 성경적인 모범 여성의 예를 잘 묘사해 주고 있습니다. 잠언 31장 10절에는 "누가 현숙한 여인을 찾아 얻겠느냐 그 값은 진주보다 더 하니라." 라고 말씀하고 있습니다. 이 말씀을 시작으로, 잠언은 현숙한 여성의 성격과 인품에 대해서 자세하게 묘사하고 있습니다. 잠언 31장에 등장하는 여인은 세상이 기준으로 삼는 여인과는 다른 성품을 가지고 있는 것처럼 보입니다.

히브리어 성경을 보면, 현숙한 여인은 *esheth hail*이라고 표현하고 있습니다. *esheth hail*이라는 표현은 문자적으로 강인한 여성이라는 뜻입니다. 성경에 나오는 사라, 드보라, 에스더와 같은 여성이 이런 강한 여성의 특징을 잘 보여줍니다. 그럼에도 불구하고, 성경은 룻에게만 *esheth hail*(룻 3:11)이라는 표현을 사용하고 있습니다.

그렇다면 룻은 어떻게 자신이 강함을 나타내고 있을까요? 우선 룻은 결정에 있어서 단호함이 있었습니다. 나오미와 함께 하기 위해 그녀는 그녀가 태어나 자랐던 고향을 떠났습니

2. Body

(1) A Biblical Woman: A Woman of Inner Strength

In the Bible, there appear many women of faith. Proverbs 31 describes especially well an exemplar woman of the Bible. In Proverbs 31:10 it is written:

> [10]*A wife of noble character who can find?*
> *She is worth far more than rubies.*

This passage describes the characteristics and personality of a virtuous woman. It seems the woman described in Proverbs 31 is not measured by worldly standards.

The Hebrew word for virtuous woman is *esheth hail*, which literally means 'strong woman'. Women of the Bible such as Sarah, Deborah, and Esther all had characteristics of a strong woman. But it is Ruth alone who, in the Bible, is referred to as *esheth hail*, or 'strong woman'.

Let us then examine how Ruth demonstrated her strength. **First**, Ruth was resolute and decisive. She left her motherland, her home, in order to accompany Naomi. In her time, once a person left her motherland, she was never

다. 당시에는 여자가 한 번 그 땅을 떠나면 다시는 돌아갈 수 없었습니다. 둘째로, 룻은 인내심을 가지고 있었습니다. 룻은 그녀의 시어머니인 나오미를 따라 그녀를 도울 사람이 아무도 없는 곳인 베들레헴으로 갔습니다. 이스라엘은 율법에 의해 이방인과의 혼인이 금지되어 있었기 때문에, 모압 사람인 룻은 그 곳에서 누구로부터도 동정을 받지 못했습니다. 그럼에도 불구하고 그녀는 그녀의 모든 고난을 잘 견뎌내었고 시어머니를 기쁨으로 섬겼으며, 추수꾼들이 추수한 이후에 이삭을 줍고 거두었습니다. 셋째로, 룻은 진정한 아름다움을 가지고 있었습니다. 그녀의 매력은 눈을 통해 드러나는 것이 아니라, 마음을 통해서 알 수 있는 것이었습니다. 내면의 강건함으로부터 나오는 그녀의 진정한 아름다움은 이방 여자인 룻이 보아스의 마음을 얻고, 다윗 왕의 증조모가 되어 예수님의 족보에 오르는 축복을 가능케 해주었습니다.

permitted to return. **Second**, Ruth was patient. She set out with her mother-in-law Naomi to Bethlehem, where she knew no one and knew not of one person from whom she could seek help. Marriage to Gentiles was forbidden according to the law in Israel. So Ruth, a Moabite, did not receive any sympathy from the Israelites. Nevertheless, she endured all her hardships, joyously served her mother-in-law, and gleaned and gathered among the sheaves what was left after the reapers. **Third**, Ruth had inner beauty. Her beauty was detectable not to the naked eye but by the heart. It was this inner beauty, spilled over from a sense of inner strength, which allowed for Ruth, a Gentile, to win the heart of Boaz and to become not only the great grandmother of King David but also be blessed to appear in the genealogy of Jesus.

(2) 룻의 성품 : 은혜와 진리로 충만함

그렇다면, 룻의 이러한 단호함과 인내, 진정한 아름다움은 어디에서 온 것일까요? 이러한 룻의 강점들은 룻의 성품으로부터 나왔습니다. 룻은 정말 친절하고 신실한 사람이었습니다. 룻의 이러한 성품들은 룻기 1장 16 - 17절에 잘 나와 있습니다. 나오미가 룻에게 나를 따르지 말고 집으로 돌아가라고 말했을 때, 룻은 다음과 같이 대답했습니다.

나로 어머니를 떠나며
어머니를 따르지 말고 돌아가라 강권하지 마옵소서
어머니께서 가시는 곳에 나도 가고
어머니께서 유숙하시는 곳에서 나도 유숙하겠나이다
어머니의 백성이 나의 백성이 되고
어머니의 하나님이 나의 하나님이 되시리니
어머니께서 죽으시는 곳에서 나도 죽어 거기 장사될 것이라
만일 내가 죽는 일 외에 어머니와 떠나면
여호와께서 내게 벌을 내리시고
더 내리시기를 원하나이다
(룻기 1:16-17)

친절하고 신실한 그녀의 성품으로부터 그녀의 단호함과 인내, 진정한 아름다움이 나타났습니다.

(2) Ruth's Character: Full of Grace and Truth

Where then did Ruth's resolute decisiveness, patience, and inner beauty come from? Such strength came from her character. Ruth was kind and faithful. When Naomi told Ruth to return home, Ruth answered as follows:

> [16] *"Don't urge me to leave you or to turn back from you.*
> *Where you go I will go, and where you stay I will stay.*
> *Your people will be my people and your God my God.*
> [17]*Where you die I will die, and there I will be buried.*
> *May the LORD deal with me, be it ever so severely,*
> *if anything but death separates you and me."*
> *(Ruth 1:16-17)*

Ruth's resolute decisiveness, patience, and inner beauty overflowed from her kind and faithful character.

(3) 친절하고 신실한 성품의 원천

그렇게 커다란 강점의 기초가 된 친절과 신실함은 어디로부터 나온 것일까요? 성경은 그러한 성품이 하나님의 선물이라고 가르쳐주고 있습니다. 요한복음 1장 17절에는 이런 말씀이 나옵니다.

율법은 모세로 말미암아 주어진 것이요
은혜와 진리는 예수 그리스도로 말미암아 온 것이라

은혜와 진리는 그리스 어로 *charis*와 *aletheia* 입니다. 이 단어들은 히브리어 *hesed*와 *ameth*에서 나온 말입니다. *Ameth*는 신실함, 진중함, 단호함, 그리고 진리를 나타내는 말이고, *hesed*는 선함, 친절함, 사랑이라는 의미로 쓰이는 말입니다. 요한복음 1장 14절에서는 예수님을 다음과 같이 묘사합니다.

말씀이 육신이 되어 우리 가운데 거하시매
우리가 그의 영광을 보니 아버지의 독생자의 영광이요
은혜와 진리가 충만하더라

(3) The Source of a Kind and Faithful Character

Where then did Ruth's kind and faithful character, which formed the foundation for her inner strength, come from? The Bible teaches us that such character is a gift from God. It is written in John 1:17:

> *[17]For the law was given through Moses;*
> *grace and truth came through Jesus Christ.*

The Greek words for grace and truth are *charis* and *aletheia* respectively, and these words originate from the Hebrew words *hesed* and *ameth*. *Hesed* refers to goodness, kindness, and love; *ameth* carries the meaning of faithfulness, gentleness, resolute decisiveness, and truth. John 1:14 gives a description of Jesus:

> *[14]The Word became flesh and made his dwelling*
> *among us. We have seen his glory,*
> *the glory of the One and Only,*
> *who came from the Father,*
> *full of grace and truth.*

다시 말해 예수님께서는 선하시고 신실하신 분이십니다. 동시에 그 선하심과 신실하심이 그분의 큰 영광입니다. 비슷한 구절이 출애굽기 34장 5 - 6절에 나옵니다. 출애굽기 33장 18절에서 모세가 주님의 영광을 보여 달라고 기도했을 때, 하나님은 출애굽기 34장 6절을 통해 당신의 영광을 나타내시고, 자신이 하나님이시며 은혜와 진리가 충만하신 분이심을 선포하십니다. 요컨대 하나님과 그의 아들 예수 그리스도는 한 하나님이시며, 진실로 선하시고 신실하신 분이십니다. 룻은 하나님의 선물로 그러한 성품들을 받은 하나님의 딸이며, 따라서 룻의 강함은 하나님의 선하시고 신실하신 성품으로 말미암은 것입니다. 그녀가 하나님으로부터 받은 가장 큰 축복은 바로 그녀의 성품입니다. 룻은 자신이 가장 약한 여성이었음에도 불구하고, 어려운 상황 속에서 하나님의 축복을 즐거워했던 하나님의 딸이었습니다.

Put simply, Jesus is kind and faithful; and at the same time, His kind and faithful character is His glory. In Exodus 33:18, Moses prays for God to show him His glory. And in Exodus 34:5-6, God manifests His glory and proclaims that He is God, full of grace and truth. Ultimately, God and His Son Jesus Christ are One. God is, in essence, kind and faithful. Ruth was a daughter of God who received such a character as a gift from God. Ruth's inner strength was a result of God's kind and faithful character that she was given. This character she received from God was her greatest blessing. Despite being a weak woman in the eyes of the world, Ruth was a daughter of God who rejoiced in God's blessings, even in the midst of difficulty.

3. 결론

오늘날 술과 담배, 최면성의 마약들로 인해 야기되어 각 나라와 세계 전체를 위협하는 사회적인 악은 우리에게 정말로 큰 위협과 고통을 줍니다. 그럼에도 불구하고 우리는 이 세상을 향해 진정한 강함을 보여주어야 하며, 그들 앞에 새로운 생명의 길을 열어주어야 합니다. 주님의 자녀로서 은혜와 진리로 충만한 우리의 성품으로 흑암을 몰아내도록 우리의 빛을 비춥시다. 은혜와 진리는 다시 말해 사랑입니다. 은혜와 진리로 가득한 사람은 사랑으로 가득한 사람이라고 말할 수 있습니다. 저는 지금 이 때에 WWCTU를 향한 하나님의 가장 큰 뜻이 하나님을 향한 사랑, 이웃을 향한 사랑, 심지어 원수를 향한 사랑의 마음을 가지고, 세상의 악을 이겨내고 예수님께 이 세상을 돌려드리는 것이라고 믿습니다. 은혜와 진리로 충만한 주님의 종으로 21세기로 뛰어드실 준비가 되셨습니까? 주님은 우리가 준비되어서 다가오는 어둠의 권세의 한복판에서 그분의 빛을 발하기를 원하고 계십니다. 하나님께서 이사야를 통해서 말씀하셨듯이 오늘날 우리를 향해서도 동일하게 말씀하고 계십니다.

3. Conclusion

Alcohol, nicotine, and other kinds of narcotic drugs have become the social evils of our time, inflicting pain and suffering in countries all around the globe. In spite of continuing threats, we must all the more show the world our true inner strength and help the world see a new path of life. Let us shine our light, as children of God, to cast away the darkness with our God-given character of grace and truth. Grace and truth combined are love. A person who is full of grace and truth is also full of love. I believe that God's will for the WWCTU at this time is to overcome the evils of the world and to turn the world back to Christ, with a heart of love for Him, for our neighbors, and for our enemies. Are you ready to go forward into the 21st century as His servants, equipped with grace and truth? God wills for us to be ready to radiate His light in the midst of the coming darkness. As God spoke to His people through Isaiah, He continues to speak the following words to His people today:

일어나라 빛을 발하라

이는 네 빛이 이르렀고

여호와의 영광이 네 위에 임하였음이니라

보라 어두움이 땅을 덮을 것이며

캄캄함이 만민을 가리우려니와

오직 여호와께서 네 위에 임하실 것이며

그 영광이 네 위에 나타나리니

나라들은 네 빛으로,

왕들은 비치는 네 광명으로 나아오리라.

(이사야 60:1-3)

[1] Arise, shine,
for your light has come,
and the glory of the LORD rises upon you.
[2]See, darkness covers the earth
and thick darkness is over the peoples,
but the LORD rises upon you
and his glory appears over you.
[3]Nations will come to your light,
and kings to the brightness of your dawn.
(Isaiah 60:1-3)

절제하는 여성이 아름답다, 나의 어머니 여귀옥 권사

김정주

어머니 여귀옥 권사님은 평생을 하루같이 복음 전도와 교회 섬김, 절제운동과 사랑의 헌신, 말씀교육에 힘쓰시면서 매일 산 순교의 삶을 사시다가 2006년 3월 20일에 천국에 입성하셨다. 어머님 회고록 요약 편집을 마치면서 어머님이 천국에 들어 가시던 마지막 모습이 너무나도 은혜로워 함께 나누려고 한다.

2006년 3월 20일 낮 12시17분. 어머님의 심장박동이 24, 23, ……, 0에 이르렀을 때, 어머님은 내게 영으로 분명하게 말씀하셨다. "정주야! 내가 부활했으니 기뻐해라." 그 말씀과 함께 어머님이 부활의 영광에 들어가신 확신이 위로부터 폭포수와 같이 임했다.

영안실로 어머님을 모시려고 시신을 따라 함께 가고 있는데, 어머님은 다시 분명하게 내 심령에 말씀하셨다. "정주야! 나는 선한 싸움을 싸우고 나의 달려갈 길을 마치고 믿

The Beauty of a Temperate Woman
— My Mother, Elderwoman Kwi Ok Yeu

Dr. Jung Joo Kim

My mother, Elderwoman Kwi Ok Yeu, lived each day like a living martyr—spreading the Gospel, serving the church, promoting the temperance movement, making sacrifices of love, and leading Bible studies—until she entered the gates of heaven on March 20, 2006. In editing my mother's memoirs, I was reminded of her last moments before ascending to heaven. I would like to leave a few words about her glorious entrance into heaven.

At 12:17 pm on March 20, 2006, my mother's heartbeat finally came to a halt. I sensed her spirit speak to my heart: "Jung Joo! Rejoice, for I have entered into the gates of heaven!" With these words, and with confirmation of my mother's glorious ascendance to heaven, my heart filled up with waterfalls of joy, sent from above.

As Mother's body was being transferred to the funeral home, again she spoke vividly to my heart: "My dear Jung Joo! I have fought the good fight, finished my race of faith, and kept my faith. Now a crown of righteousness awaits me. I urge all you my children to diligently run your race of faith." Mother's voice was so clear in my heart that I still remember it most vividly.

음을 지켰다. 이제 내게 의로운 면류관이 예비되어 있다. 너희도 믿음의 경주를 열심히 달리도록 하여라.”는 말씀이셨다. 마침 뉴질랜드에서 어머님 소천 소식을 듣고 급히 귀국하는 도중에 동생 김영훈 대성그룹 회장님으로부터 국제전화가 왔다. “어머님 고별예배에 디모데후서 4:7-8 말씀을 가지고 ‘승리의 삶’이라는 제목으로 설교 말씀을 부탁해주세요.”라고. 어머님이 내게 들려주신 바로 그 말씀이었다.

1주일 전, 어머님이 좀 위중하심을 보고 집에 돌아와서 저녁 예배시간에 조카들에게 “할머님께서 좀 많이 편찮으신 것 같구나. 할머님의 회복을 위해서 기도하자.”고 했더니 조카 의진이가 눈물을 뚝뚝 흘리면서 “할머니가 보고 싶어요. 할머니랑 놀려고 했는데…….” 하면서 옷자락이 눈물로 흠뻑 젖도록 한참을 울었다. 할머님을 사랑해서 보고 싶어하는 어린 생명들에게 어떻게 할머님의 소천 소식을 전할 수 있을까?

다음날 새벽에 도착한 김영훈 대성그룹 회장님은 어머님의 부활에 대한 확신과 함께 큰 기쁨을 하나님께서 우리에게 주신 것을 감사하면서, 그 자녀들에게도 매우 친절하게 할머님의 소천 소식을 알릴 수 있도록 먼저 함께 기도드렸다. 세 자녀들, 의한, 은진, 의진은 졸린 눈을 비비면서도

*[7]I have fought the good fight, I have finished the race,
I have kept the faith. [8]Now there is in store for me the
crown of righteousness, which the Lord, the righteous Judge,
will award to me on that day—and not only to me, but
also to all who have longed for his appearing.*
(2 Timothy 4:7-8)

My younger brother Younghoon, who was at the time on a business trip in New Zealand, had just heard the news about Mother and called me as he was boarding his plane. He said, "My dear sister, would you please request that 2 Timothy 4:7-8 be recited at Mother's funeral and that a special message titled 'A Victorious Life' be delivered also?" Younghoon mentioned the exact same Scripture verses that Mother had spoken to my heart.

Just a week before Mother passed away, I said to Younghoon's children during family worship service: "Grandma is not doing well and is in need of much prayer. Let's pray for her recovery." Five-year-old Eui Jin, with tears running down her face, responded, "I miss Grandma. I was hoping to play with her..." And she cried for a while, drenching her sleeves with her tears. Now with Mother gone, I thought to myself, *How and with what words could I possibly tell the children, who dearly loved and missed their grandmother, the news of their grandmother's death with most gentleness?*

Early the next morning, Younghoon returned home, filled with joy and assurance of Mother's entrance into heaven.

아빠가 출장에서 돌아오셨다고 기뻐서 벌떡 일어나 앉았다. 김영훈 대성그룹 회장님은 그들을 모아놓고, 할머님의 소천에 대하여 히브리서 12:1-2 말씀을 의지하여 이렇게 나누었다.

"이러므로 우리에게 구름같이 둘러싼 허다한 증인들이 있으니 모든 무거운 것과 얽매이기 쉬운 죄를 벗어 버리고 인내로써 우리 앞에 당한 경주를 경주하며" 이 말씀을 먼저 함께 읽고 어린 자녀들에게 물었다. "애들아! 운동경기장의 관중석을 가득 메운 응원단들이 경주하는 사람들을 응원하고 있는 모습을 상상해 보겠니? 할머님께서 지금 천국 스타디움의 응원단장으로 부르심을 받으셨단다. 그래서 우리들이 영적으로 큰 싸움을 할 때, 열심히 응원해주실 것이란다." 의한, 은진, 의진이는 저희 아빠가 전하는 말을 듣자마자 "할머니가 돌아가셨단 말이에요?" 하고는 울음을 터뜨렸다. 특히 의진이는 "할머니가 와서 나랑 놀아주시기를 기다렸는데……." 하면서 애통한 심정으로 울었다. 그때 아빠가 다시 물었다. "애들아! 할머님이 너희가 웃는 것을 기뻐하시겠니? 우는 것을 기뻐하시겠니?" 하고 물으니 애써 울음을 그쳤다.

온 가족들이 아침 식탁에 앉았을 때, 의한이가 큰 목소리

Before he spoke to his children about their grandmother's death, he asked that his wife and I first pray with him for guidance. Rubbing their sleepy eyes, Eui Han, Eun Jin, and young Eui Jin got out of bed to greet their father who had returned home. When his children gathered around him, Younghoon read Hebrews 12:1-2 before he began to explain to them Mother's glorious entrance into heaven.

¹Therefore, since we are surrounded by such a great cloud of witnesses, let us throw off everything that hinders and the sin that so easily entangles, and let us run with perseverance the race marked out for us.
(Hebrews 12:1)

"My dear children! Imagine a stadium filled with crowds of people, cheering on the athletes who are running their race. Well, your grandmother was chosen to lead the cheerleading squad in a stadium in heaven. We too are running a race, a race of faith. But Grandma will cheer us on whenever we face spiritual trials in our race." Immediately after Younghoon finished speaking, all three of them, asked, "Are you telling us that Grandma passed away?" as they burst into tears. Eui Jin cried most sorrowfully as she said to her father, "I was waiting for Grandma to come and play with me..." When Younghoon asked, "My dear children, when Grandma looks down from heaven, would she be happier to see you cry, or smile?" the children tried to contain their tears.

로 식사기도를 드렸다. "하나님 아버지! 우리도 할머니처럼 선한 싸움을 싸우고 달려갈 길을 마친 후 의의 면류관을 쓰게 해 주세요. 예수님 이름으로 기도합니다. 아-멘." 기도한 후 눈을 뜨더니 성령의 감동을 받아 의한이는 우렁차게 찬송을 불렀다. "행군 나팔 소리로 주의 호령 났으니 십자가의 군기를 높이 들고 나가자." 그 노래를 온 가족이 함께 따라 부르는데 어린 의진이가 식탁의자에서 벌떡 일어서더니, "선한 싸움 다 싸우고 의의 면류관, 의의 면류관, 받아 쓰리라." 라고 후렴을 크게 부르면서 아름다운 몸짓으로 춤을 추기 시작했다. 부활 신앙의 큰 기쁨이 의한, 은진, 의진에게 찾아온 것이다.

그 다음날 어머님을 기념하는 모든 장례예배, 곧 입관예배, 영락교회 장례예배, 절제회 기념예배, 돈암장 방문 예배 그리고 영락동산의 하관예배에 이르기까지 트럼펫 연주자의 반주에 맞추어 의한, 은진, 의진이는 큰 목소리로 이 찬양을 불렀다.

어머님의 소천 소식을 듣고 4일장으로 치렀던 빈소에는 2천명이 넘는 조문객들이 줄을 이었고, 부내온 조화들은 둘곳이 없도록 넘쳐나 보내신 분들의 성함을 담은 리본들이 서울대학교 영안실 큰 방과 복도 벽들을 빽빽하게 채우고

When we all sat down at the breakfast table, Eui Han prayed aloud in a loud voice: "Heavenly Father! Bless us so that we may, like Grandma, fight a good fight, run our race of faith, keep our faith, and receive the crown of righteousness. In the name of Jesus, we pray. Amen." And inspired by the Holy Spirit, he began to sing Hymn 402:

> Bugle calls are ringing out, forward is the battle shout,
> See where floats the conqu'ring sign, onward to the war divine.

All of us joined Eui Han in singing the hymn, but Eui Jin got up from her seat and began to dance, singing the refrain with utter joy:

> And when the battle's over, we shall wear a crown (3x)
> And when the battle's over, we shall wear a crown
> in the new Jerusalem.
> Wear a crown, wear a crown, away over Jordan.
> And when the battle's over, we shall wear a crown
> in the new Jerusalem.

We witnessed God's showers of joy upon the three young children at their grandmother's entrance into heaven. The next day at the four funeral services and the following ceremonies, Eui Han, Eun Jin, and Eui Jin loudly sang this hymn to the rhythm of a trumpet.

Over 2,000 guests came to the mortuary to say their last farewells to Mother. The condolence flowers we received

있었다. 빈소를 함께 지키며 모든 장례 절차에 함께 했던 친척들, 교인들, 절제회 회원들, 그리고 대성그룹 임직원들은 우리 가족들 위에 임하신 하나님의 기쁨, 곧 부활의 확신을 보면서 오히려 힘을 얻는 것을 볼 수 있었다. 장례예배가 시종 하나님께 드리는 찬양예배가 되었기 때문이다. 김영훈 장로님은 뉴질랜드에서 국제전화로 장례예배 식순을 시종 찬양예배로 드리도록 원했다. 그래서 찬송가 13장 '기뻐하며 경배하세. 영광의 주 하나님'을 회중 찬양으로 하고, 말씀은 '승리의 삶'이라는 제목으로 디모데후서 4:7-8 말씀으로, 성가대 찬양은 어머님이 생전에 늘 찬양대와 가정예배 그리고 솔로로 잘 부르시던 헨델의 메시야 '할렐루야'를 불렀다. 집전하기 위해 참여했던 영락교회 이철신 목사님과 덕수교회 손인웅 목사님은 이렇게 찬양으로 충만한 장례예배는 처음이라고 하시며, 기독교인들의 장례예배는 이렇게 감사와 찬양, 기쁨이 넘쳐야 한다고 말씀하셨다. 손인웅 목사님은 그 다음 날, 주일설교에서 이 말씀을 교인들에게 전해주심으로 천국백성의 부활의 증거를 상기시켜 주셨다.

따스한 햇살이 부드럽게 내리는 봄볕에 하관예배를 드리며 무덤 둘레에 서 있었다. 관을 내리고 흙을 덮어 드리면서

filled the Seoul National University funeral home and its hallways. I was able to witness how our family's display of confidence in God's joy and promise of resurrection strengthened hope in the hearts of our relatives, church members, KWCTU members, employees of the Daesung Group, and all others who offered our family their condolences. This was all the more possible because our funeral service turned into a worship service to God. When Younghoon called me from New Zealand, he had expressed his wishes for the funeral service to be a worship service to God. So we made arrangements to sing Hymn 13 "Joyful, Joyful, We Adore Thee" and to have a message on 2 Timothy 4:7-8 titled "A Victorious Life" delivered. Also, the church choir was asked to sing the Hallelujah Chorus from Handel's *Messiah*, which Mother often sang with the church choir, during family worship service, and as a solo. Both Pastor Chul Shin Lee of Youngnak Presbyterian Church and Pastor In Ung Son of Ducksoo Presbyterian Church mentioned how they had never been to a funeral service that was filled with so much praise and thanksgiving; that every Christian's funeral service ought to be filled with praise, thanksgiving, and overflowing joy. The next day during Sunday service, Pastor Son shared with his congregation what he had witnessed at the funeral, and his words stirred in their hearts the need to reflect upon their lives as citizens of heaven.

Standing in the spring sunshine and wrapped in the warm sunlight, we huddled around the burial site. When Mother's coffin was being lowered, and even when mounds of dirt

도 우리의 시선은 구름 한 점 없는 높은 푸른 하늘로 달려가고 있었다. 천국에서 믿음의 경주를 마치시고 의의 면류관을 쓰시고 기뻐하시는 어머님의 모습이 너무도 생생하게 영안으로 보여서, 우리 가슴에는 큰 기쁨이 흘러 넘쳤다. 모든 예배를 트럼펫 소리에 맞추어 '행군 나팔 소리로 (찬송가 402장)'를 부르고 마치면서, 모든 성도들과 우리 가족은 딤후 4:7-8 말씀대로 어머님을 본받아 믿음의 선한 싸움을 싸울 것을 다짐하고 성령의 도우심을 간절히 구하는 기도를 드렸다.

어머님은 믿음과 기도로 사시던 모습 그대로 주님 앞에 나아가셨다. 그것을 목도한 우리 자녀들에게 또 하나의 사명이 주어졌다. 어떠한 삶을 사셨길래 이렇게 영광스럽게 천국에 입성할 수 있으셨는지, 어머님께서 사시던 모습을 후손들에게 남기는 것이다.

이제 대성그룹 60주년을 맞이하여 아버지의 회고록과 함께 어머님의 자서전을 축약한 회고록의 편집을 마치고 출간하게 되어 참 감사하다. 어머님을 사랑하시는 모든 분들이 부활의 영광에 들어가신 어머님의 삶과 마지막 모습을 읽으면서, 어머님처럼 평생 산 순교의 삶과 믿음의 경주에 기쁘게 동참하게 되시기를 축복한다.

were piling atop, our eyes were fixed on the cloudless blue skies. Our hearts leaped with overflowing joy because we all could imagine Mother, who had finished her race of faith, joyously smiling with a crown of righteousness on her head. Singing along to the sound of the trumpet playing Hymn 402 "Bugle Calls are Ringing Out," the funeral service came to a close. As it says in 2 Timothy 4:7-8, our family and all the guests were reminded, once again, of how we must all fight the good fight of faith. So we offered up our fervent prayers for the Holy Spirit to be upon us on our walks of faith.

Mother went to be with the Lord as the woman of faith and prayer that she had always been. And in witnessing the faithful life that Mother lived, we her children have been given yet another mission: to pass down to our descendants Mother's inspirational life story of faith which led to her glorious entrance through the gates of heaven.

My heart overflows with thanksgiving for this blessed opportunity to condense my mother's autobiography, *Beautiful Memories*, and to release my father's and also my mother's memoirs in celebration of the 60th anniversary of the Daesung Group. May the Lord's boundless blessings be upon you who read about my mother's last moments and her glorious entrance into heaven. I hope you enjoy journeying through my mother's lifelong race of faith and her spirit of martyrdom.

● 저자 여귀옥 명예회장 약력

1923년 5월 10일   대구 출생

1941년 10월 27일   김수근 씨와 결혼

학력

1938년   대구 신명여고 졸업

1938년   평양여자신학교 수료

기관 및 학회 활동

1952년   대한기독교여자절제회 대구지회 이사

1959년   대구 절제회관 구입

1962년   대한기독교여자절제회 서울 연합회 이사

1965년   영락교회 권사 임직

          서울 절제회관 구입

1968년   주부클럽 중앙위원장

1969년   서울 절제회관 건축

1972년   대한기독교여자절제회 연합회 회장

● *About the Author: Honorary Chairwoman Kwi Ok Yeu*

10 May 1923   Born in Daegu, Korea

27 October 1941   Married Soo Keun Kim

Education

1938   Graduated from Shin Myung Girls' High School

1938   Studied at Pyeongyang Woman's Theological Seminary

Activities

1952   Trustee of the KWCTU, Daegu Chapter

1959   Purchase of the KWCTU Hall in Daegu

1962   Trustee of the KWCTU Headquarters, Seoul

1965   Appointed elderwoman at Youngnak Presbyterian Church, Seoul

Purchase of the KWCTU Hall in Seoul

1968   Director of the Wives' Club

1969   KWCTU Hall in Seoul completed

1972   President of the KWCTU

1976년   가족법개정위원회 부회장

1978년   평화통일자문위원

1980, 83, 86, 89, 95년   세계기독교여자절제회 세계대회 참석

          (영국 쉐필드, 미국 시카고, 필리핀 마닐라, 캐나다 에드먼

          턴, 호주 멜버른)

1987년   대한기독교여자절제회 대구 절제회관 건립

1992년   영락여자신학교 후원회 회장

저서

1993년   아름다운 추억 초판, 5판(2001)

1989-1997   국민일보 인터뷰 및 기고문 다수

수상 경력

1982년   여성단체협의회 회장상 수상

1976   Vice President of the Committee for the Reform of Family Law

1978   Consulting Member of the Committee on Peaceful Unification
of Korea

1980, 83, 86, 89, 95

Delegate at the Triennial World Convention of the WWCTU

(Sheffield, England; Chicago, USA; Manila, Philippines;

Edmonton, Canada; and Melbourne, Australia)

1987   KWCTU Hall in Daegu completed

1992   President of Patrons, Youngnak Woman's Theological
Seminary

Books and Articles

1993   *Walking After the Light: Beautiful Memories*

(Korean edition, 1st print); 5th print (2001)

1989-1997   Articles and interviews in "Kukmin Daily
Newspaper"

Prize

1982   Recipient of the Prize of President of the National
Council of Women

● 편집자 김정주 박사 약력

1949년   10월 20일 대구 출생

학력

1972   이화여대 영어영문학 학사 (BA)

1973   미국 University of Michigan 영문학 석사(MA)

1980   미국 Fuller Theological Seminary 선교학 석사 (MA)

1989   미국 Harvard University 신약학 박사 (ThD)

연구 및 논문

1989   (Harvard University)

The Spirit of God as Witness to the Redemption in Christ: A Tradition-Historical Analysis of Paul's Pneumatology in Romans 8

● *About the Editor: Dr. Jung Joo Kim*

20 October 1949   Born in Daegu, Korea

Education

1972   BA in English Literature, Ewha Woman's University, Korea

1973   MA in English Literature, University of Michigan, USA

1980   MA in Mission and Evangelism, Fuller Theological Seminary, USA

1989   ThD, Harvard University, USA

Thesis

1989   (Harvard University)

The Spirit of God as Witness to the Redemption in Christ: A Tradition-Historical Analysis of Paul's Pneumatology in Romans 8

저서 및 역서

1997   바울의 성령 이해

편저

1993   절제운동 70년사

1998   빛을 따라 걸었더니: 아름다운 추억 (영문판)

2003   일어나라 빛을 발하라.

2004   죽음을 이겨낸 영원한 삶 (*More Than Conquerors:*
       주기철 목사님 순교기)

2005   *My Cup Overflows* (손양원 목사님 순교기)

2006   *The Royal Way* (잠언 한 · 일 · 영 · 중 4개 국어 대조판)

기관 및 학회 활동

1994 – 현재 연세대학교 교수

1997 – 현재 대한기독교여자절제회 연합회 부회장

1992 – 1998 세계기독교여자절제회 (WWCTU) 세계 수석 부회장

2003 – 현재 대성닷컴 (Daesung.Com) 사장

2004 – 현재 세계기독교여자절제회 (WWCTU) 세계 수석 부회장

Books

1997   *Paul's Pneumatology* (Korean Edition)

Books Edited

1993   *70 Year History of the KWCTU*

1998   *Walking After the Light: Beautiful Memories* (English Edition)

2003   *Arise and Shine!*

2004   *More Than Conquerors*

2005   *My Cup Overflows*

2006   *The Royal Way*

Activities

1994-present   Professor, Yonsei University

1997-present   Vice President, KWCTU

1992-1998   World Vice President, WWCTU

2003-present   President, Daesung.com

2004-present   World Vice President, WWCTU

빛을 따라 걸었더니
아름다운 추억

초판 인쇄 | 2007년 5월 1일
초판 발행 | 2007년 5월 10일

발행처 | 대성닷컴(주) JCR
발행인 | 김영훈

등록번호 | 제300-2003-82호
등록일자 | 2003년 5월 6일

서울시 종로구 관훈동 151-8 동덕빌딩 11층 대성닷컴(주)
대표전화 | (02)3700-1764
팩스 | (02)3700-1701
www.daesungbook.com   jcrbooks@korea.com

ISBN 978-89-958974-3-0
ISBN 978-89-958974-4-7(세트)
ⓒ대성닷컴(주) JCR 2007

정가 9,500원

본서에 인용한 성경 본문은 특별한 표기가 없는 한 성경전서 개역개정판을 사용하였습니다.

Walking After the Light
Beautiful Memories

JCR. DAESUNG.COM CO., LTD.
11th fl. Dongduk Bldg. 151-8 Gwanhun-dong Jongno-gu
Seoul, 110-300 Korea
Tel +82 2 3700 1764   Fax +82 2 3700 1701
www.daesungbook.com   jcrbooks@korea.com

ISBN 978-89-958974-3-0
ISBN 978-89-958974-4-7(Set)
ⓒDaesung.com Co., Ltd., JCR 2007

All Scripture is taken from the New International Version (NIV) unless otherwise stated.

Printed in Korea